WARSHIPS 1860–1970

WARSHIPS 1860–1970

A COLLECTION OF NAVAL LORE

J M THORNTON

ARCO PUBLISHING COMPANY, INC.
New York

Published 1973 by Arco Publishing Company, Inc
219 Park Avenue South, New York, N.Y. 10003

ISBN 0 668 033193
Library of Congress Catalog Card Number 73 79068

Printed in Great Britain

Contents

Preface

This collection of drawings is presented as a unique record of a most exciting period of naval history — the last 100 years. The illustrations trace the development and deployment of modern warships, highlighting some of the less well-known incidents and facets that make the subject so fascinating.

The drawings originally appeared in the Royal Canadian Navy's now defunct magazine *Crowsnest* over a period of 15 years. Many were reprinted in the British Navy League's magazine *Sea Cadet*, the Indian Navy's magazine *Varuna*, and the South African military paper *Kommando*, as well as other publications in Canada and the USA.

Originally entitled '*Naval Lore Corner*', the original drawings have been re-assembled and edited, some discarded and new ones added in order to present a logical sequence to a series of self-contained illustrated articles.

PART ONE

The New Age

With the approach of the twentieth century and the age of super-technology, the navies of the world underwent a great metamorphosis. Iron and steel replaced seasoned oak and acres of canvas gave way to ponderous reciprocating engines. Broadside muzzle-loading cannons were succeeded by central batteries and turreted breach-loaders. For thirty years the designers and builders vied with each other to produce the optimum warship types, and within a quarter of a century 20,000 ton dreadnoughts ruled the oceans, their mighty guns capable of vastly greater fire-power than all the old wooden-walls combined.

By the middle of the present century the monster steel battleships which had ruled supreme for such a short span of history had all but disappeared, superseded by aircraft carriers, missles and nuclear submarines.

SAIL-POWER DIED HARD IN
THE ROYAL NAVY. UNTIL ABOUT
1885, ALL IRONCLADS WERE
EQUIPPED WITH MASTS AND
YARDS TO SUPPLEMENT THEIR
ENGINES. SEVERAL OF THESE
SHIPS WERE "MODERNIZED",
LOSING THEIR SAILING CAPACITY
IN THE PROCESS...

H.M.S. MONARCH (1869)... THE FIRST
BRITISH SEA-GOING TURRET SHIP AND
THE FIRST BRITISH WARSHIP TO MOUNT
12-INCH GUNS WAS ORIGINALLY DESIGNED
AS A FULL-RIGGED SHIP AND LATER RE-
FITTED WITH BARQUE-RIG (ABOVE).
THE RIGGING SERIOUSLY HAMPERED HER
GUNFIRE AND IN 1890 SHE WAS TAKEN
IN HAND FOR MODERNIZATION. SEVEN
YEARS LATER SHE RECOMMISSIONED
(RIGHT) EQUIPPED WITH MILITARY MASTS,
A TALLER FUNNEL, VENTILATORS AND A
CHART-HOUSE. SHE WAS ALSO RE-
ENGINED. ODDLY ENOUGH, HER OLD
MUZZLE-LOADING GUNS WERE RETAINED!

H.M.S. SULTAN (1871)... A BROADSIDE BATTLESHIP,
WAS DESIGNED WITH FULL-SHIP RIG, BUT
WAS REDUCED TO A BARQUE (ABOVE) IN 1876.
IN 1889 SHE GROUNDED AND SANK AT
MALTA, WAS RAISED AND MODERNIZED
(LEFT) AT PORTSMOUTH. SHE RE-COM-
MISSIONED IN 1896 WITH 2 TALL FUNNELS,
MILITARY MASTS, COWLS, NEW ENGINES AND
A DOUBLE BRIDGE. HOWEVER, THE OLD SHIP
WAS NOT WORTH THE "MODERNIZATION"
AND PROVED OF QUESTIONABLE VALUE...

J.M. THORNTON

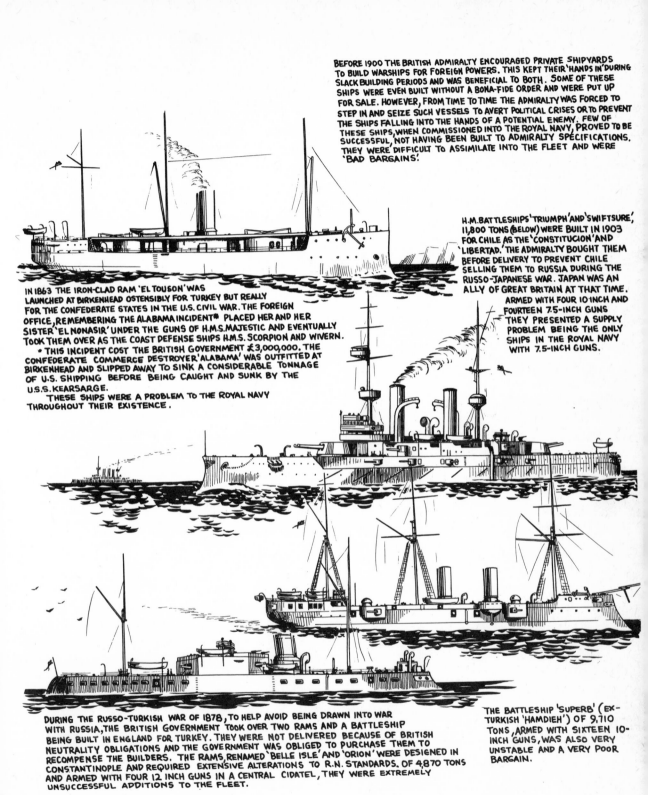

BEFORE 1900 THE BRITISH ADMIRALTY ENCOURAGED PRIVATE SHIPYARDS TO BUILD WARSHIPS FOR FOREIGN POWERS. THIS KEPT THEIR 'HANDS IN' DURING SLACK BUILDING PERIODS AND WAS BENEFICIAL TO BOTH. SOME OF THESE SHIPS WERE EVEN BUILT WITHOUT A BONA-FIDE ORDER AND WERE PUT UP FOR SALE. HOWEVER, FROM TIME TO TIME THE ADMIRALTY WAS FORCED TO STEP IN AND SEIZE SUCH VESSELS TO AVERT POLITICAL CRISES OR TO PREVENT THE SHIPS FALLING INTO THE HANDS OF A POTENTIAL ENEMY. FEW OF THESE SHIPS, WHEN COMMISSIONED INTO THE ROYAL NAVY, PROVED TO BE SUCCESSFUL, NOT HAVING BEEN BUILT TO ADMIRALTY SPECIFICATIONS. THEY WERE DIFFICULT TO ASSIMILATE INTO THE FLEET AND WERE 'BAD BARGAINS'.

H.M.BATTLESHIPS 'TRIUMPH' AND 'SWIFTSURE', 11,800 TONS (BELOW) WERE BUILT IN 1903 FOR CHILE AS THE 'CONSTITUCION' AND 'LIBERTAD'. THE ADMIRALTY BOUGHT THEM BEFORE DELIVERY TO PREVENT CHILE SELLING THEM TO RUSSIA DURING THE RUSSO-JAPANESE WAR. JAPAN WAS AN ALLY OF GREAT BRITAIN AT THAT TIME.
ARMED WITH FOUR 10 INCH AND FOURTEEN 7.5-INCH GUNS THEY PRESENTED A SUPPLY PROBLEM BEING THE ONLY SHIPS IN THE ROYAL NAVY WITH 7.5-INCH GUNS.

IN 1863 THE IRON-CLAD RAM 'EL TOUSON' WAS LAUNCHED AT BIRKENHEAD OSTENSIBLY FOR TURKEY BUT REALLY FOR THE CONFEDERATE STATES IN THE U.S. CIVIL WAR. THE FOREIGN OFFICE, REMEMBERING THE ALABAMA INCIDENT* PLACED HER AND HER SISTER 'EL NONASIR' UNDER THE GUNS OF H.M.S. MAJESTIC AND EVENTUALLY TOOK THEM OVER AS THE COAST DEFENSE SHIPS H.M.S. SCORPION AND WIVERN.

* THIS INCIDENT COST THE BRITISH GOVERNMENT £3,000,000. THE CONFEDERATE COMMERCE DESTROYER 'ALABAMA' WAS OUTFITTED AT BIRKENHEAD AND SLIPPED AWAY TO SINK A CONSIDERABLE TONNAGE OF U.S. SHIPPING BEFORE BEING CAUGHT AND SUNK BY THE U.S.S. KEARSARGE.

THESE SHIPS WERE A PROBLEM TO THE ROYAL NAVY THROUGHOUT THEIR EXISTENCE.

DURING THE RUSSO-TURKISH WAR OF 1878, TO HELP AVOID BEING DRAWN INTO WAR WITH RUSSIA, THE BRITISH GOVERNMENT TOOK OVER TWO RAMS AND A BATTLESHIP BEING BUILT IN ENGLAND FOR TURKEY. THEY WERE NOT DELIVERED BECAUSE OF BRITISH NEUTRALITY OBLIGATIONS AND THE GOVERNMENT WAS OBLIGED TO PURCHASE THEM TO RECOMPENSE THE BUILDERS. THE RAMS, RENAMED 'BELLE ISLE' AND 'ORION' WERE DESIGNED IN CONSTANTINOPLE AND REQUIRED EXTENSIVE ALTERATIONS TO R.N. STANDARDS. OF 4,870 TONS AND ARMED WITH FOUR 12 INCH GUNS IN A CENTRAL CIDATEL, THEY WERE EXTREMELY UNSUCCESSFUL ADDITIONS TO THE FLEET.

THE BATTLESHIP 'SUPERB' (EX-TURKISH 'HAMDIEH') OF 9,710 TONS, ARMED WITH SIXTEEN 10-INCH GUNS, WAS ALSO VERY UNSTABLE AND A VERY POOR BARGAIN.

J.M. THORNTON

By 1885 naval designers were no longer concerned with the fitting of tall masts and yards. The accommodation of machinery spaces, boiler rooms and bunkerage created new problems and the great masted men-of-war of an earlier, more romantic, era gave way to multi-funnelled steel vessels with guns of unprecedented power.

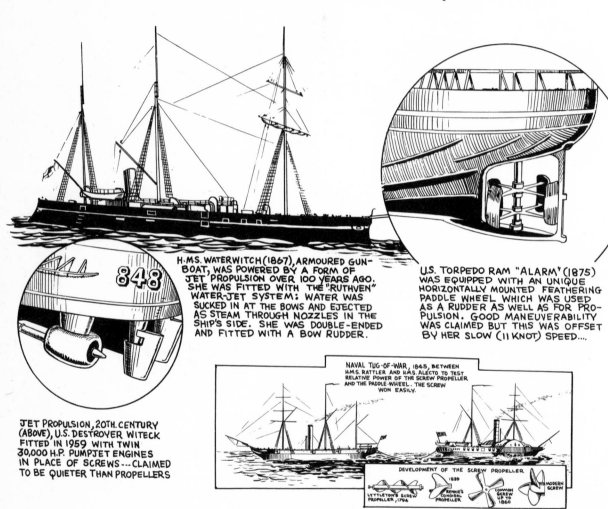

H.M.S. WATERWITCH (1867), ARMOURED GUN-BOAT, WAS POWERED BY A FORM OF JET PROPULSION OVER 100 YEARS AGO. SHE WAS FITTED WITH THE "RUTHVEN" WATER-JET SYSTEM: WATER WAS SUCKED IN AT THE BOWS AND EJECTED AS STEAM THROUGH NOZZLES IN THE SHIP'S SIDE. SHE WAS DOUBLE-ENDED AND FITTED WITH A BOW RUDDER.

U.S. TORPEDO RAM "ALARM" (1875) WAS EQUIPPED WITH AN UNIQUE HORIZONTALLY MOUNTED FEATHERING PADDLE WHEEL WHICH WAS USED AS A RUDDER AS WELL AS FOR PRO-PULSION. GOOD MANEUVERABILITY WAS CLAIMED BUT THIS WAS OFFSET BY HER SLOW (11 KNOT) SPEED....

JET PROPULSION, 20TH. CENTURY (ABOVE), U.S. DESTROYER WITECK FITTED IN 1959 WITH TWIN 30,000 H.P. PUMPJET ENGINES IN PLACE OF SCREWS --- CLAIMED TO BE QUIETER THAN PROPELLERS

NAVAL TUG-OF-WAR, 1845, BETWEEN H.M.S. RATTLER AND H.M.S. ALECTO TO TEST RELATIVE POWER OF THE SCREW PROPELLER AND THE PADDLE-WHEEL. THE SCREW WON EASILY.

DEVELOPMENT OF THE SCREW PROPELLER

LYTTLETON'S SCREW PROPELLER, 1794

RENNIE'S CONOIDAL PROPELLER 1839

COMMON SCREW UP TO 1860

MODERN SCREW

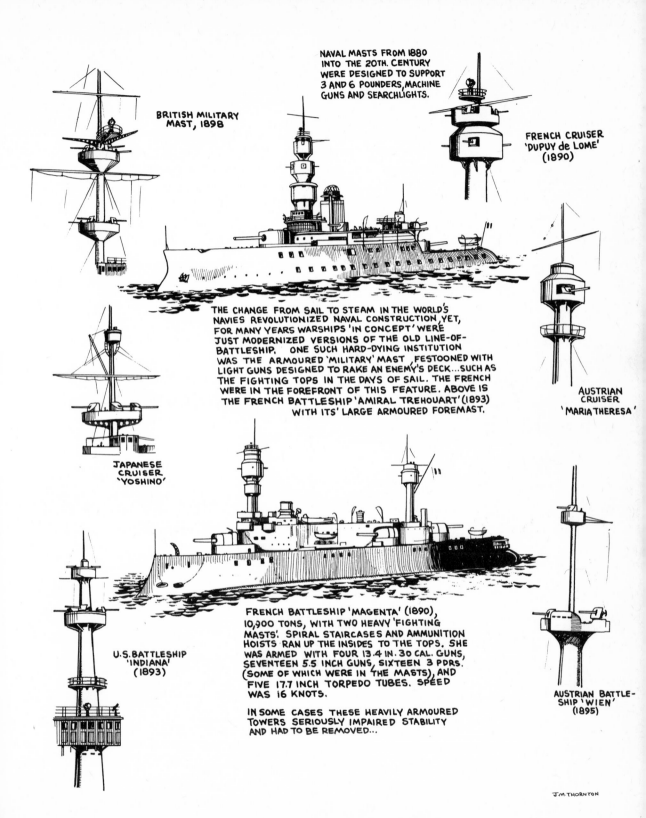

NAVAL MASTS FROM 1880
INTO THE 20TH. CENTURY
WERE DESIGNED TO SUPPORT
3 AND 6 POUNDERS, MACHINE
GUNS AND SEARCHLIGHTS.

BRITISH MILITARY
MAST, 1898

FRENCH CRUISER
'DUPUY de LOME'
(1890)

THE CHANGE FROM SAIL TO STEAM IN THE WORLD'S
NAVIES REVOLUTIONIZED NAVAL CONSTRUCTION, YET,
FOR MANY YEARS WARSHIPS 'IN CONCEPT' WERE
JUST MODERNIZED VERSIONS OF THE OLD LINE-OF-
BATTLESHIP. ONE SUCH HARD-DYING INSTITUTION
WAS THE ARMOURED 'MILITARY' MAST, FESTOONED WITH
LIGHT GUNS DESIGNED TO RAKE AN ENEMY'S DECK...SUCH AS
THE FIGHTING TOPS IN THE DAYS OF SAIL. THE FRENCH
WERE IN THE FOREFRONT OF THIS FEATURE. ABOVE IS
THE FRENCH BATTLESHIP 'AMIRAL TREHOUART' (1893)
WITH ITS' LARGE ARMOURED FOREMAST.

AUSTRIAN
CRUISER
'MARIA THERESA'

JAPANESE
CRUISER
'YOSHINO'

FRENCH BATTLESHIP 'MAGENTA' (1890),
10,900 TONS, WITH TWO HEAVY 'FIGHTING
MASTS'. SPIRAL STAIRCASES AND AMMUNITION
HOISTS RAN UP THE INSIDES TO THE TOPS. SHE
WAS ARMED WITH FOUR 13.4 IN. 30 CAL. GUNS,
SEVENTEEN 5.5 INCH GUNS, SIXTEEN 3 PDRS.
(SOME OF WHICH WERE IN THE MASTS), AND
FIVE 17.7 INCH TORPEDO TUBES. SPEED
WAS 16 KNOTS.

IN SOME CASES THESE HEAVILY ARMOURED
TOWERS SERIOUSLY IMPAIRED STABILITY
AND HAD TO BE REMOVED...

U.S. BATTLESHIP
'INDIANA'
(1893)

AUSTRIAN BATTLE-
SHIP 'WIEN'
(1895)

J.M.THORNTON

13

RUSSIAN BATTLESHIP "NAVARIN" (1891) (ABOVE), WAS FITTED WITH TWO PAIRS OF FUNNELS. SHE WAS SUNK AT TSUSHIMA IN 1905...

FRENCH BATTLESHIP "CARNOT" (1894) (LEFT) HAD A SQUARE DOUBLE FORE FUNNEL. ON 12,150 TONS SHE CARRIED TWO 12-INCH GUNS, TWO 10.8-INCH GUNS, AND EIGHT 5.5-INCH GUNS...

RUSSIAN CRUISER "ASKOLD" (1900) HAD FIVE FUNNELS AND WAS NICKNAMED "THE PACKAGE OF WOODBINES" BY THE BRITISH. SHE LED A VERY CHECKERED CAREER DURING THE FIRST WAR AND AT ONE TIME WAS SEIZED BY THE ROYAL NAVY...

ITALIAN BATTLESHIP "SARDEGNA" (1890) (ABOVE) HAD HER TWO FORWARD FUNNELS MOUNTED ABREAST. SHE WAS ARMED WITH FOUR 13.5-INCH GUNS...

U.S. GUNBOAT "NASHVILLE" (1895) (1,371 TONS) HAD THE TALLEST FUNNELS IN PROPORTION TO THE SIZE OF VESSEL OF ANY NAVAL VESSEL. ARMAMENT WAS EIGHT 4-INCH GUNS...

FRENCH ARMOURED CRUISER "ERNEST RENAN" (1906) HAD SIX FUNNELS TRUNKED FROM WIDELY SEPARATED BOILER ROOMS — A DESIGN FEATURE THAT WAS FAVOURED IN THE FRENCH AND ITALIAN NAVIES. SHE CARRIED FOUR 7.6-INCH GUNS AND TWELVE 6.4-INCH GUNS (13,644 TONS).

FUNNEL ARRANGEMENTS TO KEEP FUMES CLEAR OF BRIDGES AND TO CONSERVE SPACE

BRITISH 'DARING' CLASS DESTROYERS, 1952-4... FOREFUNNEL ENCASED IN LATTICE FOREMAST.

JAPANESE BATTLESHIP "NAGATO" (1920) HAD FORE FUNNEL BENT REARWARD IN 1924. IN 1936 BOTH FUNNELS WERE COMBINED...

RUSSIAN BATTLESHIPS OF 'SEVASTOPOL' CLASS (1911), FORE FUNNEL BENT REARWARD...

BRITISH BATTLESHIP "WARSPITE" (1913) AFTER HER FIRST REFIT WITH HER TWO FUNNELS TRUNKED TOGETHER

U.S. GUIDED MISSILE DE- STROYERS 'BELKNAP' CLASS (1963-65) FITTED WITH "MACKS" (COMBINED MASTS AND STACKS)...

①. THE OLD WOODEN-WALLS MOUNTED THEIR GUNS IN ROWS ON THEIR GUN DECKS, EACH FIRING THROUGH ITS OWN GUN-PORT. THEY COULD NOT BE AIMED, THE SHIP HAVING TO LAY ALONGSIDE ITS ADVERSARY TO DELIVER A BROADSIDE...

②. AN EARLY ATTEMPT TO INCORPORATE SOME DEGREE OF AXIAL FIRE WAS ATTEMPTED IN HMS RESEARCH (1864). THE HULL SIDES BEFORE AND ABAFT THE BOX BATTERY WERE RECESSED AND GUN-PORTS CUT IN THE BULKHEADS THROUGH WHICH THE TRAVERSED GUNS COULD ALSO BE POINTED TOWARDS THE BOW AND STERN...

③. THE AFTER 7-INCH GUN OF HMS DEFENCE (RE-ARMED 1867) WAS MOUNTED ON AN ELABORATE SYSTEM OF TRACKS SO THAT IT COULD BE FIRED THROUGH 2 STERN PORTS, AND ONE ON EACH QUARTER...

⑤ HMS HOTSPUR (1871) THE ONLY SHIP TO HAVE A FIXED TURRET. HER SINGLE 25-TON GUN WAS MOUNTED IN A FIXED TURRET PIERCED BY 4 GUN-PORTS. THIS PROVED SINGULARLY UNSUCCESSFUL...

④ HMS MONARCH (1869)...THE FIRST BRITISH SEA-GOING TURRET SHIP. HER FOUR 12-INCH GUNS WERE MOUNTED IN 2 MIDSHIP TURRETS...BUT THE OLD "BROADSIDE" CONCEPT DIED HARD, AND THESE GUNS COULD STILL NOT FIRE AHEAD OR ASTERN, BUT ONLY IN LIMITED ARCS ON EITHER BEAM...

⑥ HMS CERBERUS (1870)..THE FIRST BRITISH WARSHIP WITH A CENTRAL SUPERSTRUCTURE AND FORE AND AFT TURRETS. A MONITOR OF 3,340 TONS, SHE CARRIED FOUR 10-INCH 'MLR' GUNS AT 9.75 KNOTS. SHE PROVED THAT A FEW TURRET GUNS WERE MORE EFFECTIVE THAN MANY FIXED BROADSIDE GUNS. SHE WAS THE FORERUNNER OF THE 20TH CENTURY BATTLESHIP.

J.M.THORNTON

THE EVOLUTION OF THE BIG-GUN TURRET...

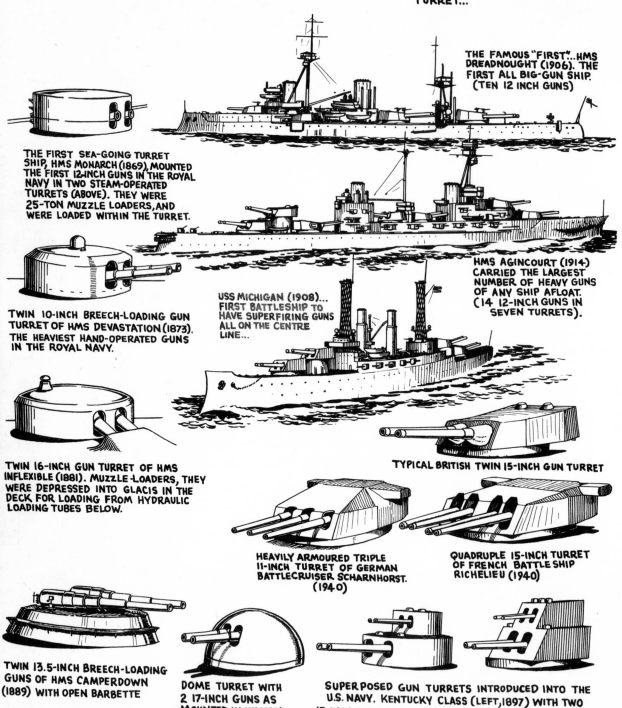

THE FAMOUS "FIRST"...HMS DREADNOUGHT (1906). THE FIRST ALL BIG-GUN SHIP. (TEN 12 INCH GUNS)

THE FIRST SEA-GOING TURRET SHIP, HMS MONARCH (1869), MOUNTED THE FIRST 12-INCH GUNS IN THE ROYAL NAVY IN TWO STEAM-OPERATED TURRETS (ABOVE). THEY WERE 25-TON MUZZLE LOADERS, AND WERE LOADED WITHIN THE TURRET.

TWIN 10-INCH BREECH-LOADING GUN TURRET OF HMS DEVASTATION (1873). THE HEAVIEST HAND-OPERATED GUNS IN THE ROYAL NAVY.

HMS AGINCOURT (1914) CARRIED THE LARGEST NUMBER OF HEAVY GUNS OF ANY SHIP AFLOAT. (14 12-INCH GUNS IN SEVEN TURRETS).

USS MICHIGAN (1908)... FIRST BATTLESHIP TO HAVE SUPERFIRING GUNS ALL ON THE CENTRE LINE...

TWIN 16-INCH GUN TURRET OF HMS INFLEXIBLE (1881). MUZZLE-LOADERS, THEY WERE DEPRESSED INTO GLACIS IN THE DECK FOR LOADING FROM HYDRAULIC LOADING TUBES BELOW.

TYPICAL BRITISH TWIN 15-INCH GUN TURRET

HEAVILY ARMOURED TRIPLE 11-INCH TURRET OF GERMAN BATTLECRUISER SCHARNHORST. (1940)

QUADRUPLE 15-INCH TURRET OF FRENCH BATTLESHIP RICHELIEU (1940)

TWIN 13.5-INCH BREECH-LOADING GUNS OF HMS CAMPERDOWN (1889) WITH OPEN BARBETTE

DOME TURRET WITH 2 17-INCH GUNS AS MOUNTED IN ITALIAN BATTLESHIP RUGGIERO DI LAURIA (1884)

SUPERPOSED GUN TURRETS INTRODUCED INTO THE U.S. NAVY. KENTUCKY CLASS (LEFT, 1897) WITH TWO 13-INCH GUNS AND TWO 8-INCH GUNS AND NEW JERSEY CLASS (RIGHT) WITH TWO 12-INCH GUNS AND TWO 8-INCH GUNS.

J.M.THORNTON

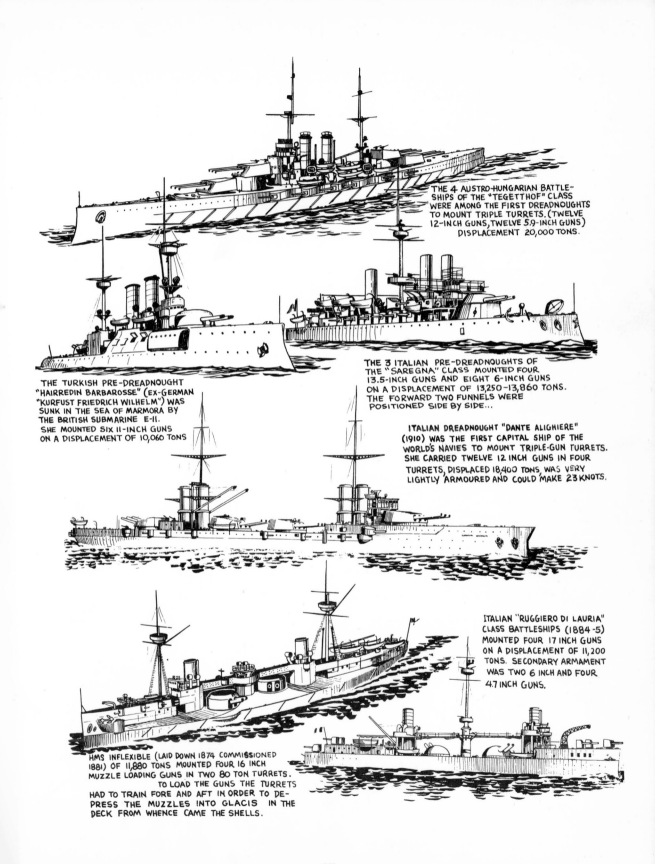

THE 4 AUSTRO-HUNGARIAN BATTLE-
SHIPS OF THE "TEGETTHOF" CLASS
WERE AMONG THE FIRST DREADNOUGHTS
TO MOUNT TRIPLE TURRETS. (TWELVE
12-INCH GUNS, TWELVE 5.9-INCH GUNS)
DISPLACEMENT 20,000 TONS.

THE 3 ITALIAN PRE-DREADNOUGHTS OF
THE "SAREGNA" CLASS MOUNTED FOUR
13.5-INCH GUNS AND EIGHT 6-INCH GUNS
ON A DISPLACEMENT OF 13,250-13,860 TONS.
THE FORWARD TWO FUNNELS WERE
POSITIONED SIDE BY SIDE...

THE TURKISH PRE-DREADNOUGHT
"HAIRREDIN BARBAROSSE" (EX-GERMAN
"KURFUST FRIEDRICH WILHELM") WAS
SUNK IN THE SEA OF MARMORA BY
THE BRITISH SUBMARINE E-II.
SHE MOUNTED SIX 11-INCH GUNS
ON A DISPLACEMENT OF 10,060 TONS

ITALIAN DREADNOUGHT "DANTE ALIGHIERE"
(1910) WAS THE FIRST CAPITAL SHIP OF THE
WORLD'S NAVIES TO MOUNT TRIPLE-GUN TURRETS.
SHE CARRIED TWELVE 12 INCH GUNS IN FOUR
TURRETS, DISPLACED 18,400 TONS, WAS VERY
LIGHTLY ARMOURED AND COULD MAKE 23 KNOTS.

ITALIAN "RUGGIERO DI LAURIA"
CLASS BATTLESHIPS (1884-5)
MOUNTED FOUR 17 INCH GUNS
ON A DISPLACEMENT OF 11,200
TONS. SECONDARY ARMAMENT
WAS TWO 6 INCH AND FOUR
4.7 INCH GUNS.

HMS INFLEXIBLE (LAID DOWN 1874 COMMISSIONED
1881) OF 11,880 TONS MOUNTED FOUR 16 INCH
MUZZLE LOADING GUNS IN TWO 80 TON TURRETS.
TO LOAD THE GUNS THE TURRETS
HAD TO TRAIN FORE AND AFT IN ORDER TO DE-
PRESS THE MUZZLES INTO GLACIS IN THE
DECK FROM WHENCE CAME THE SHELLS.

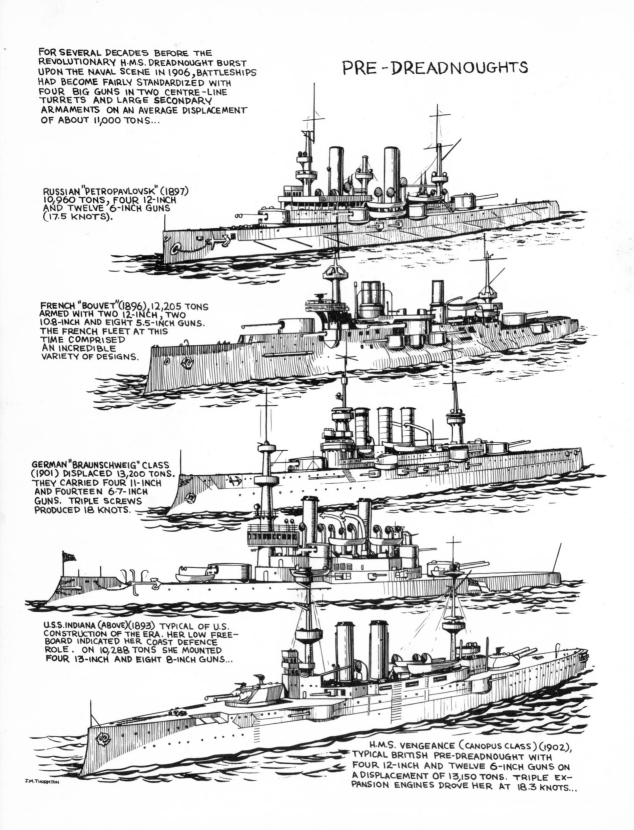

FOR SEVERAL DECADES BEFORE THE
REVOLUTIONARY H.M.S. DREADNOUGHT BURST
UPON THE NAVAL SCENE IN 1906, BATTLESHIPS
HAD BECOME FAIRLY STANDARDIZED WITH
FOUR BIG GUNS IN TWO CENTRE-LINE
TURRETS AND LARGE SECONDARY
ARMAMENTS ON AN AVERAGE DISPLACEMENT
OF ABOUT 11,000 TONS...

PRE-DREADNOUGHTS

RUSSIAN "PETROPAVLOVSK" (1897)
10,960 TONS, FOUR 12-INCH
AND TWELVE 6-INCH GUNS
(17.5 KNOTS).

FRENCH "BOUVET"(1896), 12,205 TONS
ARMED WITH TWO 12-INCH, TWO
10.8-INCH AND EIGHT 5.5-INCH GUNS.
THE FRENCH FLEET AT THIS
TIME COMPRISED
AN INCREDIBLE
VARIETY OF DESIGNS.

GERMAN "BRAUNSCHWEIG" CLASS
(1901) DISPLACED 13,200 TONS.
THEY CARRIED FOUR 11-INCH
AND FOURTEEN 6.7-INCH
GUNS. TRIPLE SCREWS
PRODUCED 18 KNOTS.

U.S.S. INDIANA (ABOVE)(1893) TYPICAL OF U.S.
CONSTRUCTION OF THE ERA. HER LOW FREE-
BOARD INDICATED HER COAST DEFENCE
ROLE. ON 10,288 TONS SHE MOUNTED
FOUR 13-INCH AND EIGHT 8-INCH GUNS...

J.M. THORNTON

H.M.S. VENGEANCE (CANOPUS CLASS) (1902),
TYPICAL BRITISH PRE-DREADNOUGHT WITH
FOUR 12-INCH AND TWELVE 6-INCH GUNS ON
A DISPLACEMENT OF 13,150 TONS. TRIPLE EX-
PANSION ENGINES DROVE HER AT 18.3 KNOTS...

THE CLASSIFICATION OF WARSHIPS IN
MODERN NAVIES INTO DISTINCT TYPES
HAS BECOME MORE AND MORE OBSCURE.
UP TO THE END OF WORLD WAR II,
HOWEVER, WARSHIPS FELL INTO SEVERAL
ESTABLISHED CATEGORIES. THERE WERE,
HOWEVER, SOME EXCEPTIONS WHICH HAD
THE CHARACTERISTICS OF MORE THAN
ONE TYPE.....

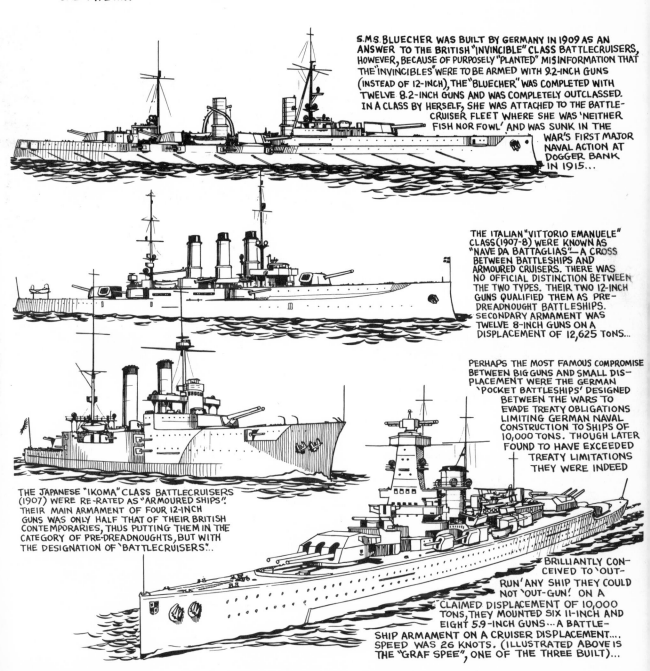

S.M.S. BLUECHER WAS BUILT BY GERMANY IN 1909 AS AN
ANSWER TO THE BRITISH "INVINCIBLE" CLASS BATTLECRUISERS,
HOWEVER, BECAUSE OF PURPOSELY "PLANTED" MISINFORMATION THAT
THE "INVINCIBLES" WERE TO BE ARMED WITH 9.2-INCH GUNS
(INSTEAD OF 12-INCH), THE "BLUECHER" WAS COMPLETED WITH
TWELVE 8.2-INCH GUNS AND WAS COMPLETELY OUTCLASSED.
IN A CLASS BY HERSELF, SHE WAS ATTACHED TO THE BATTLE-
CRUISER FLEET WHERE SHE WAS 'NEITHER
FISH NOR FOWL' AND WAS SUNK IN THE
WAR'S FIRST MAJOR
NAVAL ACTION AT
DOGGER BANK
IN 1915...

THE ITALIAN "VITTORIO EMANUELE"
CLASS (1907-8) WERE KNOWN AS
"NAVE DA BATTAGLIAS"—A CROSS
BETWEEN BATTLESHIPS AND
ARMOURED CRUISERS. THERE WAS
NO OFFICIAL DISTINCTION BETWEEN
THE TWO TYPES. THEIR TWO 12-INCH
GUNS QUALIFIED THEM AS PRE-
DREADNOUGHT BATTLESHIPS.
SECONDARY ARMAMENT WAS
TWELVE 8-INCH GUNS ON A
DISPLACEMENT OF 12,625 TONS...

PERHAPS THE MOST FAMOUS COMPROMISE
BETWEEN BIG GUNS AND SMALL DIS-
PLACEMENT WERE THE GERMAN
'POCKET BATTLESHIPS' DESIGNED
BETWEEN THE WARS TO
EVADE TREATY OBLIGATIONS
LIMITING GERMAN NAVAL
CONSTRUCTION TO SHIPS OF
10,000 TONS. THOUGH LATER
FOUND TO HAVE EXCEEDED
TREATY LIMITATIONS
THEY WERE INDEED

THE JAPANESE "IKOMA" CLASS BATTLECRUISERS
(1907) WERE RE-RATED AS "ARMOURED SHIPS".
THEIR MAIN ARMAMENT OF FOUR 12-INCH
GUNS WAS ONLY HALF THAT OF THEIR BRITISH
CONTEMPORARIES, THUS PUTTING THEM IN THE
CATEGORY OF PRE-DREADNOUGHTS, BUT WITH
THE DESIGNATION OF 'BATTLECRUISERS'...

BRILLIANTLY CON-
CEIVED TO 'OUT-
RUN' ANY SHIP THEY COULD
NOT 'OUT-GUN'! ON A
CLAIMED DISPLACEMENT OF 10,000
TONS, THEY MOUNTED SIX 11-INCH AND
EIGHT 5.9-INCH GUNS... A BATTLE-
SHIP ARMAMENT ON A CRUISER DISPLACEMENT....
SPEED WAS 26 KNOTS. (ILLUSTRATED ABOVE IS
THE "GRAF SPEE", ONE OF THE THREE BUILT)...

J. M. THORNTON

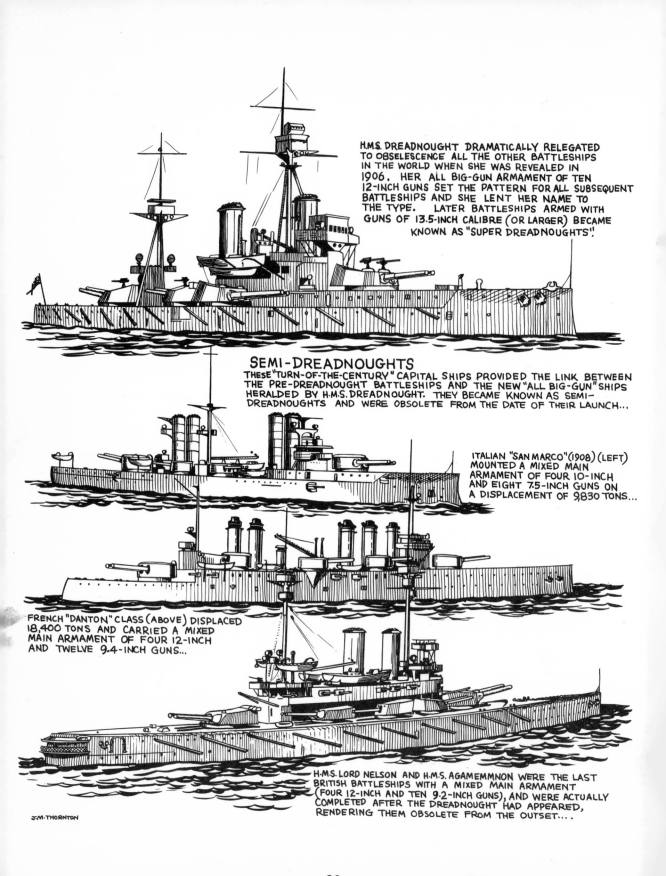

H.M.S. DREADNOUGHT DRAMATICALLY RELEGATED
TO OBSELESCENCE ALL THE OTHER BATTLESHIPS
IN THE WORLD WHEN SHE WAS REVEALED IN
1906. HER ALL BIG-GUN ARMAMENT OF TEN
12-INCH GUNS SET THE PATTERN FOR ALL SUBSEQUENT
BATTLESHIPS AND SHE LENT HER NAME TO
THE TYPE. LATER BATTLESHIPS ARMED WITH
GUNS OF 13.5-INCH CALIBRE (OR LARGER) BECAME
KNOWN AS "SUPER DREADNOUGHTS".

SEMI-DREADNOUGHTS
THESE "TURN-OF-THE-CENTURY" CAPITAL SHIPS PROVIDED THE LINK BETWEEN
THE PRE-DREADNOUGHT BATTLESHIPS AND THE NEW "ALL BIG-GUN" SHIPS
HERALDED BY H.M.S. DREADNOUGHT. THEY BECAME KNOWN AS SEMI-
DREADNOUGHTS AND WERE OBSOLETE FROM THE DATE OF THEIR LAUNCH...

ITALIAN "SAN MARCO" (1908) (LEFT)
MOUNTED A MIXED MAIN
ARMAMENT OF FOUR 10-INCH
AND EIGHT 7.5-INCH GUNS ON
A DISPLACEMENT OF 9,830 TONS...

FRENCH "DANTON" CLASS (ABOVE) DISPLACED
18,400 TONS AND CARRIED A MIXED
MAIN ARMAMENT OF FOUR 12-INCH
AND TWELVE 9.4-INCH GUNS...

J·M·THORNTON

H.M.S. LORD NELSON AND H.M.S. AGAMEMNON WERE THE LAST
BRITISH BATTLESHIPS WITH A MIXED MAIN ARMAMENT
(FOUR 12-INCH AND TEN 9.2-INCH GUNS), AND WERE ACTUALLY
COMPLETED AFTER THE DREADNOUGHT HAD APPEARED,
RENDERING THEM OBSOLETE FROM THE OUTSET....

THE RISE & FALL OF THE BATTLECRUISER

CONCEIVED AT THE TURN OF THE CENTURY, THE BATTLECRUISER WAS TO BE A CAPITAL SHIP, EQUAL IN POWER TO A BATTLESHIP, BUT SACRIFICING ARMOUR FOR SPEED. HER FUNCTION IN A FLEET ACTION WAS, BY VIRTUE OF HER SUPERIOR SPEED, TO OVERTAKE THE ENEMY BATTLEFLEET & ENGAGE UNTIL HER OWN BATTLEFLEET ARRIVED.

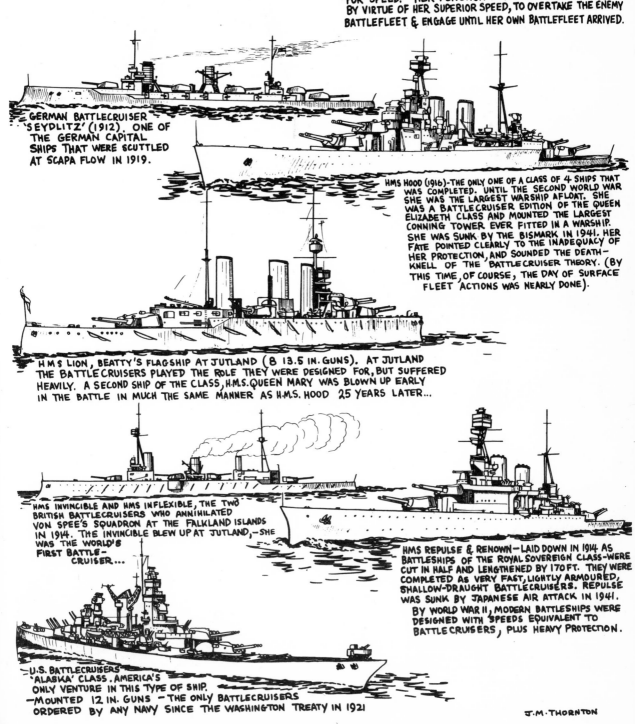

GERMAN BATTLECRUISER 'SEYDLITZ' (1912). ONE OF THE GERMAN CAPITAL SHIPS THAT WERE SCUTTLED AT SCAPA FLOW IN 1919.

HMS HOOD (1916) - THE ONLY ONE OF A CLASS OF 4 SHIPS THAT WAS COMPLETED. UNTIL THE SECOND WORLD WAR SHE WAS THE LARGEST WARSHIP AFLOAT. SHE WAS A BATTLECRUISER EDITION OF THE QUEEN ELIZABETH CLASS AND MOUNTED THE LARGEST CONNING TOWER EVER FITTED IN A WARSHIP. SHE WAS SUNK BY THE BISMARK IN 1941. HER FATE POINTED CLEARLY TO THE INADEQUACY OF HER PROTECTION, AND SOUNDED THE DEATH-KNELL OF THE BATTLECRUISER THEORY. (BY THIS TIME, OF COURSE, THE DAY OF SURFACE FLEET ACTIONS WAS NEARLY DONE).

HMS LION, BEATTY'S FLAGSHIP AT JUTLAND (8 13.5 IN. GUNS). AT JUTLAND THE BATTLECRUISERS PLAYED THE ROLE THEY WERE DESIGNED FOR, BUT SUFFERED HEAVILY. A SECOND SHIP OF THE CLASS, H.M.S. QUEEN MARY WAS BLOWN UP EARLY IN THE BATTLE IN MUCH THE SAME MANNER AS H.M.S. HOOD 25 YEARS LATER...

HMS INVINCIBLE AND HMS INFLEXIBLE, THE TWO BRITISH BATTLECRUISERS WHO ANNIHILATED VON SPEE'S SQUADRON AT THE FALKLAND ISLANDS IN 1914. THE INVINCIBLE BLEW UP AT JUTLAND, - SHE WAS THE WORLD'S FIRST BATTLE-CRUISER...

HMS REPULSE & RENOWN — LAID DOWN IN 1914 AS BATTLESHIPS OF THE ROYAL SOVEREIGN CLASS — WERE CUT IN HALF AND LENGTHENED BY 170 FT. THEY WERE COMPLETED AS VERY FAST, LIGHTLY ARMOURED, SHALLOW-DRAUGHT BATTLECRUISERS. REPULSE WAS SUNK BY JAPANESE AIR ATTACK IN 1941.

BY WORLD WAR II, MODERN BATTLESHIPS WERE DESIGNED WITH SPEEDS EQUIVALENT TO BATTLECRUISERS, PLUS HEAVY PROTECTION.

~ U.S. BATTLECRUISERS 'ALASKA' CLASS. AMERICA'S ONLY VENTURE IN THIS TYPE OF SHIP.
— MOUNTED 12 IN. GUNS — THE ONLY BATTLECRUISERS ORDERED BY ANY NAVY SINCE THE WASHINGTON TREATY IN 1921

J.M. THORNTON

BONUS for the BATTLEFLEET

AT THE START OF WORLD WAR I THERE WERE SEVERAL WARSHIPS BUILDING IN BRITISH YARDS FOR FOREIGN GOVERNMENTS, INCLUDING THREE BATTLESHIPS... ALL OF WHICH WERE TAKEN OVER BY THE ADMIRALTY AT THE COMMENCEMENT OF HOSTILITIES. THESE VESSELS, BUILT TO FOREIGN SPECIFICATIONS, FORMED AN ODD BUT VALUABLE ADDITION TO THE GRAND FLEET. ALL FOUGHT AT JUTLAND, AND ONLY ONE EVENTUALLY SERVED ITS ORIGINAL OWNERS...

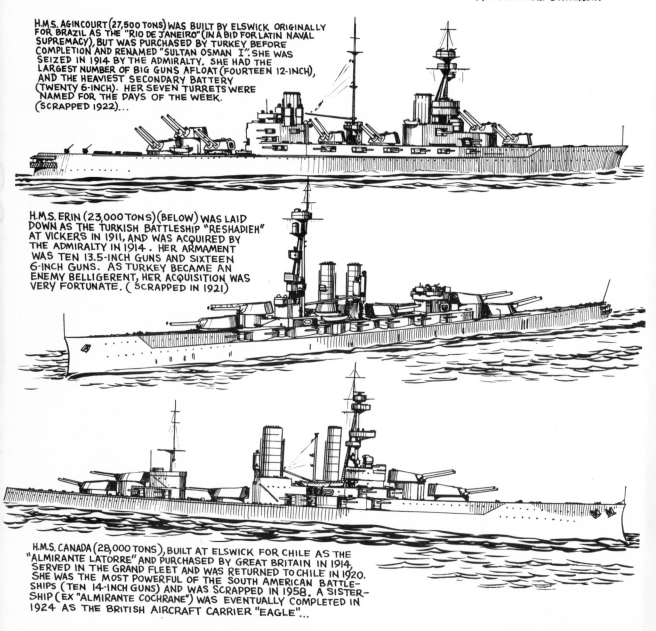

H.M.S. AGINCOURT (27,500 TONS) WAS BUILT BY ELSWICK ORIGINALLY FOR BRAZIL AS THE "RIO DE JANEIRO" (IN A BID FOR LATIN NAVAL SUPREMACY), BUT WAS PURCHASED BY TURKEY BEFORE COMPLETION AND RENAMED "SULTAN OSMAN I". SHE WAS SEIZED IN 1914 BY THE ADMIRALTY. SHE HAD THE LARGEST NUMBER OF BIG GUNS AFLOAT (FOURTEEN 12-INCH), AND THE HEAVIEST SECONDARY BATTERY (TWENTY 6-INCH). HER SEVEN TURRETS WERE NAMED FOR THE DAYS OF THE WEEK. (SCRAPPED 1922)...

H.M.S. ERIN (23,000 TONS) (BELOW) WAS LAID DOWN AS THE TURKISH BATTLESHIP "RESHADIEH" AT VICKERS IN 1911, AND WAS ACQUIRED BY THE ADMIRALTY IN 1914. HER ARMAMENT WAS TEN 13.5-INCH GUNS AND SIXTEEN 6-INCH GUNS. AS TURKEY BECAME AN ENEMY BELLIGERENT, HER ACQUISITION WAS VERY FORTUNATE. (SCRAPPED IN 1921)

H.M.S. CANADA (28,000 TONS), BUILT AT ELSWICK FOR CHILE AS THE "ALMIRANTE LATORRE" AND PURCHASED BY GREAT BRITAIN IN 1914, SERVED IN THE GRAND FLEET AND WAS RETURNED TO CHILE IN 1920. SHE WAS THE MOST POWERFUL OF THE SOUTH AMERICAN BATTLE-SHIPS (TEN 14-INCH GUNS) AND WAS SCRAPPED IN 1958. A SISTER-SHIP (EX "ALMIRANTE COCHRANE") WAS EVENTUALLY COMPLETED IN 1924 AS THE BRITISH AIRCRAFT CARRIER "EAGLE"...

J.M. THORNTON

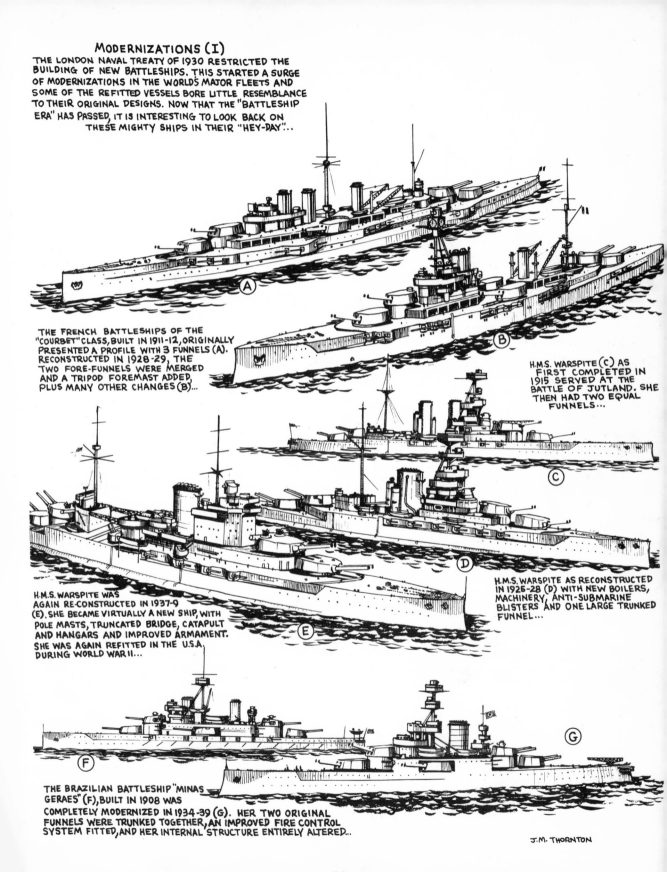

MODERNIZATIONS (I)

THE LONDON NAVAL TREATY OF 1930 RESTRICTED THE
BUILDING OF NEW BATTLESHIPS. THIS STARTED A SURGE
OF MODERNIZATIONS IN THE WORLDS MAJOR FLEETS AND
SOME OF THE REFITTED VESSELS BORE LITTLE RESEMBLANCE
TO THEIR ORIGINAL DESIGNS. NOW THAT THE "BATTLESHIP
ERA" HAS PASSED, IT IS INTERESTING TO LOOK BACK ON
THESE MIGHTY SHIPS IN THEIR "HEY-DAY"...

THE FRENCH BATTLESHIPS OF THE
"COURBET" CLASS, BUILT IN 1911-12, ORIGINALLY
PRESENTED A PROFILE WITH 3 FUNNELS (A).
RECONSTRUCTED IN 1928-29, THE
TWO FORE-FUNNELS WERE MERGED
AND A TRIPOD FOREMAST ADDED,
PLUS MANY OTHER CHANGES (B)...

H.M.S. WARSPITE (C) AS
FIRST COMPLETED IN
1915 SERVED AT THE
BATTLE OF JUTLAND. SHE
THEN HAD TWO EQUAL
FUNNELS...

H.M.S. WARSPITE WAS
AGAIN RE-CONSTRUCTED IN 1937-9
(E). SHE BECAME VIRTUALLY A NEW SHIP, WITH
POLE MASTS, TRUNCATED BRIDGE, CATAPULT
AND HANGARS AND IMPROVED ARMAMENT.
SHE WAS AGAIN REFITTED IN THE U.S.A.
DURING WORLD WAR II...

H.M.S. WARSPITE AS RECONSTRUCTED
IN 1925-28 (D) WITH NEW BOILERS,
MACHINERY, ANTI-SUBMARINE
BLISTERS AND ONE LARGE TRUNKED
FUNNEL...

THE BRAZILIAN BATTLESHIP "MINAS
GERAES" (F), BUILT IN 1908 WAS
COMPLETELY MODERNIZED IN 1934-39 (G). HER TWO ORIGINAL
FUNNELS WERE TRUNKED TOGETHER, AN IMPROVED FIRE CONTROL
SYSTEM FITTED, AND HER INTERNAL STRUCTURE ENTIRELY ALTERED...

J.M. THORNTON

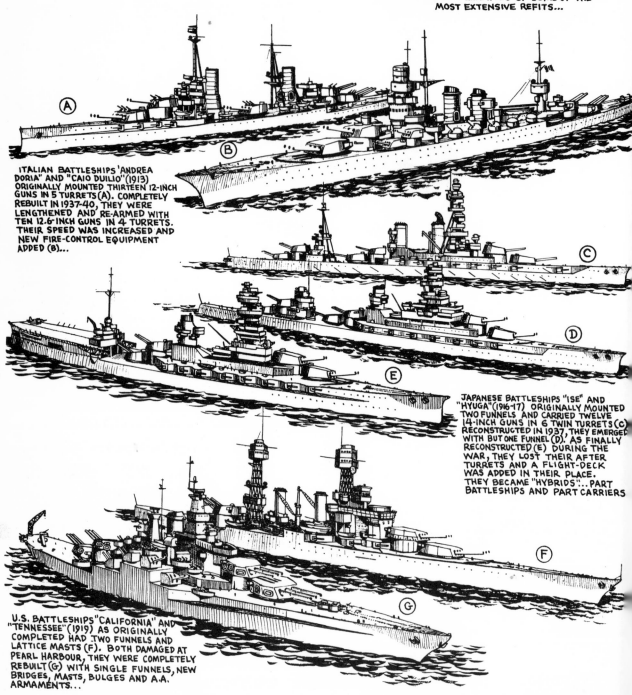

MODERNIZATIONS (II)

BEFORE AND DURING THE WAR, SOME OF THE WORLD'S LARGEST BATTLESHIPS WERE COMPLETELY REBUILT AND GIVEN A "NEW LEASE OF LIFE". DEPICTED HERE ARE EXAMPLES OF SOME OF THE MOST EXTENSIVE REFITS...

ITALIAN BATTLESHIPS "ANDREA DORIA" AND "CAIO DUILIO" (1913) ORIGINALLY MOUNTED THIRTEEN 12-INCH GUNS IN 5 TURRETS (A). COMPLETELY REBUILT IN 1937-40, THEY WERE LENGTHENED AND RE-ARMED WITH TEN 12.6-INCH GUNS IN 4 TURRETS. THEIR SPEED WAS INCREASED AND NEW FIRE-CONTROL EQUIPMENT ADDED (B)...

JAPANESE BATTLESHIPS "ISE" AND "HYUGA" (1916-17) ORIGINALLY MOUNTED TWO FUNNELS AND CARRIED TWELVE 14-INCH GUNS IN 6 TWIN TURRETS (C). RECONSTRUCTED IN 1937, THEY EMERGED WITH BUT ONE FUNNEL (D). AS FINALLY RECONSTRUCTED (E) DURING THE WAR, THEY LOST THEIR AFTER TURRETS AND A FLIGHT-DECK WAS ADDED IN THEIR PLACE. THEY BECAME "HYBRIDS"... PART BATTLESHIPS AND PART CARRIERS

U.S. BATTLESHIPS "CALIFORNIA" AND "TENNESSEE" (1919) AS ORIGINALLY COMPLETED HAD TWO FUNNELS AND LATTICE MASTS (F). BOTH DAMAGED AT PEARL HARBOUR, THEY WERE COMPLETELY REBUILT (G) WITH SINGLE FUNNELS, NEW BRIDGES, MASTS, BULGES AND A.A. ARMAMENTS...

J. M. THORNTON

PART TWO

The Fleet Takes Wings

The introduction of heavier-than-aircraft as an adjunct to the fleet had slow beginnings. At first the new-fangled aircraft were only considered for their reconnaisance value, but their impact received dramatic impetus during two World Wars. The naval staffs evolved various methods of accommodating aircraft in the ships of the fleet and from these primitive beginnings evolved the mighty aircraft carriers of the mid-twentieth century.

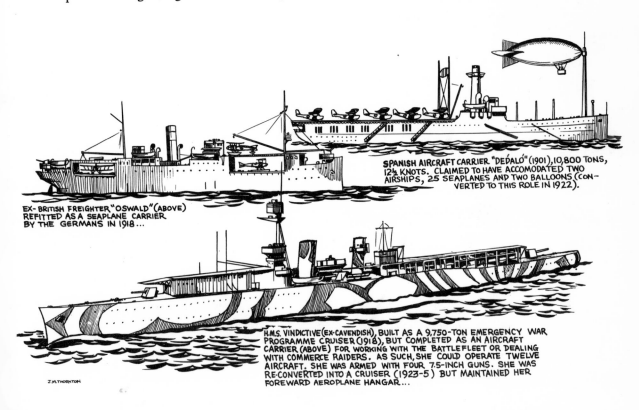

SPANISH AIRCRAFT CARRIER "DEDALO" (1901), 10,800 TONS, 12½ KNOTS. CLAIMED TO HAVE ACCOMODATED TWO AIRSHIPS, 25 SEAPLANES AND TWO BALLOONS (CONVERTED TO THIS ROLE IN 1922).

EX-BRITISH FREIGHTER "OSWALD" (ABOVE) REFITTED AS A SEAPLANE CARRIER BY THE GERMANS IN 1918...

H.M.S. VINDICTIVE (EX-CAVENDISH), BUILT AS A 9,750-TON EMERGENCY WAR PROGRAMME CRUISER (1918), BUT COMPLETED AS AN AIRCRAFT CARRIER (ABOVE) FOR WORKING WITH THE BATTLEFLEET OR DEALING WITH COMMERCE RAIDERS. AS SUCH, SHE COULD OPERATE TWELVE AIRCRAFT. SHE WAS ARMED WITH FOUR 7.5-INCH GUNS. SHE WAS RE-CONVERTED INTO A CRUISER (1923-5) BUT MAINTAINED HER FOREWARD AEROPLANE HANGAR...

J.M.THORNTON

WITH THE INTRODUCTION OF AIRCRAFT TO THE
ARSENALS OF THE WORLD, IT WAS NOT LONG
BEFORE PIONEER ATTEMPTS WERE MADE TO
OPERATE AEROPLANES FROM SHIPS. SOME OF
THESE ATTEMPTS WERE SUCCESSFUL... WHILE
OTHERS ENDED IN DISASTER...

ON 18 JANUARY, 1911, EUGENE ELY, FLYING A CURTISS
BIPLANE, MADE THE FIRST DECK-LANDING IN HISTORY...
ONTO A 130×30 FOOT PLATFORM FITTED TO THE QUARTER-
DECK OF THE U.S. CRUISER "PENNSYLVANIA" WHILE THE
SHIP WAS MOORED. HE LANDED DOWN-WIND, AND THEN
TURNED THE AIRCRAFT AROUND AND FLEW OFF OVER
THE STERN.

IN DECEMBER 1912, LT. SAMSON, R.N., TOOK OFF
FROM A LAUNCHING PLATFORM BUILT ON THE
FOC'SL OF H.M.S. AFRICA, ANCHORED AT CHATHAM,
IN A SHORT BIPLANE, AND SUCCESSFULLY LANDED
ALONGSIDE USING FLOTATION BAGS LASHED
TO THE AIRCRAFT'S UNDERCARRIAGE...

ON 3, AUGUST, 1917, SQUADRON-CDR. E.H. DUNNING,
D.S.C., R.N.A.S., MADE THE FIRST DECK-LANDING ON A
BRITISH WARSHIP UNDER WAY. HE FLEW HIS SOP-
WITH "PUP" ALONG THE SIDE OF THE GIANT CRUISER
"FURIOUS", THEN SIDE-SLIPPED ONTO A "FLYOFF" PLAT-
FORM ON THE FOC'SL, WHERE HIS FRIENDS LITERALLY
PULLED HIM DOWN. THE NEXT DAY HE ATTEMPTED
TO REPEAT THE FEAT UN-ASSISTED. A TIRE
BURST ON TOUCH-DOWN AND HE WAS KILLED...

ON 4 MAY, 1912, CDR. C.R. SAMSON, R.N., MADE THE FIRST
FLIGHT FROM A WARSHIP UNDER WAY. FLYING A SHORT
S-38 AIRCRAFT, HE TOOK OFF FROM A TEMPORARY
FLIGHT RUNWAY FITTED TO THE BATTLESHIP "HIBERNIA"
WHILE THE SHIP WAS STEAMING AT 10½ KNOTS DURING
A REVIEW OF THE FLEET BY KING GEORGE V...

J.M. THORNTON

THE BRAINCHILDREN OF LORD FISHER, 3 EXTRAORDINARY SHIPS WERE BUILT IN SECRECY IN 1914 TO OPERATE IN THE SHALLOW BALTIC IN SUPPORT OF ALLIED ARMIES. THEY WERE CALLED "LARGE LIGHT CRUISERS"...SURELY AN UNDERSTATEMENT FOR VESSELS DISPLACING NEARLY 23,000 TONS! THEY MOUNTED A FEW ENORMOUS GUNS, WERE VERY FAST AND LIGHTLY ARMOURED. THE CAMPAIGN FOR WHICH THEY WERE DESIGNED NEVER MATERIALIZED AND THEY BECAME THE 'WHITE ELEPHANTS' OF THE FLEET. TOO LIGHTLY PROTECTED TO JOIN THE BATTLE CRUISER SQUADRON, THE ADMIRALTY COULD FIND LITTLE EMPLOYMENT FOR THEM...

H.M.S. GLORIOUS AND H.M.S. COURAGEOUS AS ORIGINALLY COMPLETED, CARRIED FOUR 15-INCH GUNS AND 18 4-INCH GUNS IN TRIPLE MOUNTS AT 32 KNOTS. COURAGEOUS WAS EMPLOYED FOR A TIME AS A MINELAYER!

BOTH GLORIOUS AND COURAGEOUS WERE CONVERTED INTO AIRCRAFT CARRIERS IN 1924 (ABOVE). THE FORMER WAS SUNK BY THE GNEISENAU AND SCHARNHORST OFF NARVIK IN 1940, AND THE LATTER BY A U-BOAT IN 1939.

H.M.S. FURIOUS, THE 3RD. MEMBER OF THE TRIO, WAS DESIGNED TO CARRY TWO 18-INCH GUNS (THE LARGEST AFLOAT), BUT WAS COMPLETED WITH A 'FLYING-OFF DECK' FORWARD IN PLACE OF ONE OF THE GUNS. SHE WAS THE FIRST WARSHIP TO BE CONVERTED INTO A CARRIER. IN 1918 THE AFTER GUN WAS REPLACED BY A HANGAR AND 'FLY-ON' DECK (A). HER AIRCRAFT SUCCESSFULLY ATTACKED THE GERMAN TONDERN AIR SHIP STATION, BUT HER LANDING-ON CASUALTIES WERE SO HIGH THAT IN 1921-25 SHE WAS COMPLETELY ALTERED WITH A FULL FLIGHT DECK (B). SHE WAS SCRAPPED IN 1949.

H.M.S. FURIOUS (SHOWN HERE AS SHE WAS REBUILT FOR THE SECOND TIME IN 1918). AIRCRAFT "LANDED ON" ON THE AFTER DECK AND TOOK OFF FROM THE "FLY OFF" PLATFORM FORWARD. SMALL TROLLEYS ON BOTH SIDES OF THE SUPERSTRUCTURE TRANSFERRED THE AIRCRAFT FROM THE "FLY ON" TO THE "FLY OFF" PLATFORMS.

AS WORLD WAR I PROGRESSED, THE ROYAL NAVY'S
INTEREST IN AIRCRAFT INCREASED, AND MANY
EXPERIMENTS TOOK PLACE IN THE OPERATION OF
AIRCRAFT AT SEA. BY 1918, MOST OF THE HEAVY
GRAND FLEET SHIPS CARRIED AIRCRAFT, AND
THE FIRST AIRCRAFT CARRIERS HAD APPEARED...

ONE OF THE FIRST SEAPLANE CARRIERS WAS H.M.S. 'SLINGER'
(1917), EQUIPPED WITH A LAUNCHING CATAPULT ON THE
FOC'SL (ABOVE). A CONVERTED DREDGER, SHE WAS EMPLOYED
ON EXPERIMENTAL WORK...

IN 1918 THE ROYAL NAVY EXPERIMENTED IN FLYING OFF A
SOPWITH 'CAMEL' FROM A LIGHTER TOWED BY A DESTROYER
AT 36 KNOTS (RIGHT). LATER IN THE WAR, THIS
METHOD ENABLED THE SHORT-RANGED AIRCRAFT TO
ATTACK GERMAN ZEPPELIN BASES....

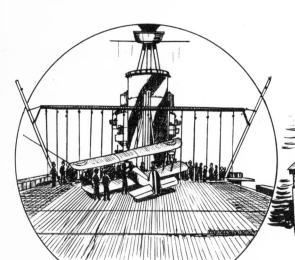

EARLY DECK LANDINGS ON H.M.S. 'FURIOUS' WERE HAZARD-
OUS AFFAIRS. AFTER HER SECOND CONVERSION, SHE STILL
RETAINED HER 'MIDSHIPS' SUPERSTRUCTURE, AND A ROPE
BARRIER WAS ERECTED ABAFT THE FUNNEL TO STOP AIR-
CRAFT THAT WERE NOT ARRESTED BY THE "FORE AND AFT"
GUIDE WIRES (FOREGROUND) AS THEY LANDED ON, OVER
THE STERN....

H.M.S. ARGUS (ABOVE) WAS THE WORLD'S FIRST FLUSH-
DECKED AIRCRAFT CARRIER, MAKING DECK LANDINGS
RELATIVELY SAFE (NOTE PALISADES ON FLIGHT
DECK). CONVERTED FROM THE HALF-COMPLETED
LINER "CONTE ROSSO", SHE COMMISSIONED IN SEPT.,
1918, TOO LATE FOR OPERATIONS IN WORLD WAR I.
SHE SERVED IN WORLD WAR II, AND WAS
SCRAPPED IN 1947...

J.M. THORNTON

IN WORLD WAR I, AS THE IMPORTANCE OF AIRCRAFT INCREASED, VARIOUS METHODS WERE INTRODUCED TO CARRY AIRCRAFT WITH THE FLEET. BY 1918 NEARLY ALL BATTLESHIPS AND LARGE CRUISERS CARRIED 1 OR 2 AIRCRAFT, AND SEVERAL SHIPS WERE SPECIALLY CONVERTED AS THE FIRST AIRCRAFT CARRIERS...

H.M.S. ARK ROYAL (RIGHT), LAID DOWN AS A COLLIER, BECAME THE FIRST AIRCRAFT CARRIER. SEAPLANES STOWED IN HER HOLDS WERE LOWERED OVER THE SIDE BY CRANES IN ORDER TO TAKE OFF FROM THE WATER.

H.M.S. CAMPANIA (BELOW), A CONVERTED CUNARDER HAD HER FORE-FUNNEL DIVIDED IN 1916 TO PROVIDE A LONGER FLYING-OFF PLATFORM. SHE WAS SUNK IN COLLISION SHORTLY AFTER THE WAR.

H.M.S. MANXMAN (ABOVE) WAS TYPICAL OF SEVERAL CONFINED SEAS PACKETS CONVERTED INTO CARRIERS (1915). A SISTERSHIP, H.M.S. ENGADINE SENT UP THE ONLY AIRPLANE TO PARTICIPATE IN THE BATTLE OF JUTLAND. IT SIGHTED THE HIGH SEAS FLEET...

H.M.S. ARGUS (ABOVE), LAID DOWN AS THE LINER "CONTE ROSSO" FOR ITALY WAS COMPLETED IN 1918 AS A CARRIER...TOO LATE FOR THE WAR. SHE HAD THE FIRST COMPLETE FLIGHT DECK, ENABLING AIRCRAFT TO FLY ON WITH SOME DEGREE OF SAFETY. HER WHEELHOUSE (A) COULD BE LOWERED FLUSH WITH THE DECK WHEN OPERATING AIRCRAFT. SHE WAS SCRAPPED IN 1947...

H.M.S. HERMES (LAUNCHED 1919) WAS THE FIRST SHIP DESIGNED AS A CARRIER. OF 10,850 TONS, SHE COULD ACCOMMODATE 20 AIRCRAFT. HER DESIGN PROVIDED THE PATTERN FOR ALL SUBSEQUENT CARRIERS. SHE WAS SUNK BY THE JAPANESE IN 1942...

J. M. THORNTON

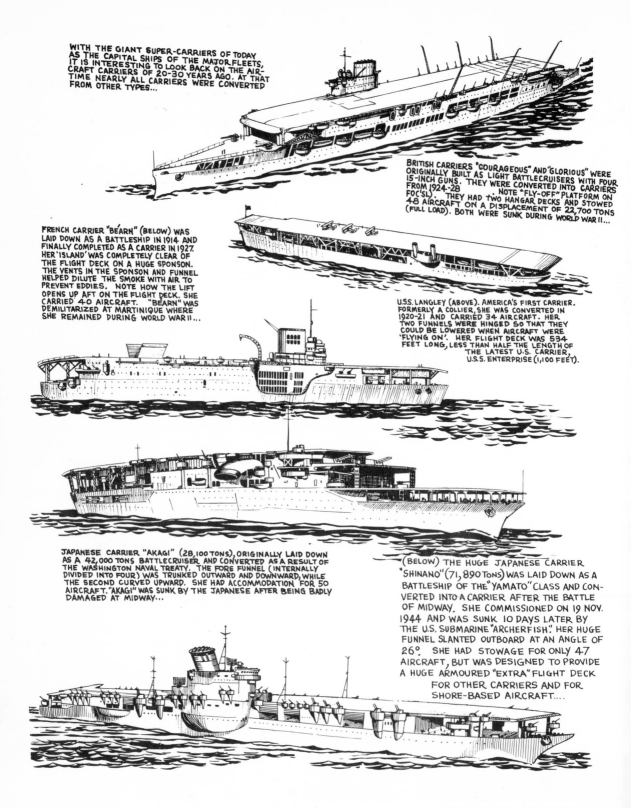

WITH THE GIANT SUPER-CARRIERS OF TODAY AS THE CAPITAL SHIPS OF THE MAJOR FLEETS, IT IS INTERESTING TO LOOK BACK ON THE AIR-CRAFT CARRIERS OF 20-30 YEARS AGO. AT THAT TIME NEARLY ALL CARRIERS WERE CONVERTED FROM OTHER TYPES...

BRITISH CARRIERS "COURAGEOUS" AND "GLORIOUS" WERE ORIGINALLY BUILT AS LIGHT BATTLECRUISERS WITH FOUR 15-INCH GUNS. THEY WERE CONVERTED INTO CARRIERS FROM 1924-28. NOTE "FLY-OFF" PLATFORM ON FOC'SL. THEY HAD TWO HANGAR DECKS AND STOWED 48 AIRCRAFT ON A DISPLACEMENT OF 22,700 TONS (FULL LOAD). BOTH WERE SUNK DURING WORLD WAR II...

FRENCH CARRIER "BÉARN" (BELOW) WAS LAID DOWN AS A BATTLESHIP IN 1914 AND FINALLY COMPLETED AS A CARRIER IN 1927. HER "ISLAND" WAS COMPLETELY CLEAR OF THE FLIGHT DECK ON A HUGE SPONSON. THE VENTS IN THE SPONSON AND FUNNEL HELPED DILUTE THE SMOKE WITH AIR TO PREVENT EDDIES. NOTE HOW THE LIFT OPENS UP AFT ON THE FLIGHT DECK. SHE CARRIED 40 AIRCRAFT. "BÉARN" WAS DEMILITARIZED AT MARTINIQUE WHERE SHE REMAINED DURING WORLD WAR II...

U.S.S. LANGLEY (ABOVE). AMERICA'S FIRST CARRIER. FORMERLY A COLLIER, SHE WAS CONVERTED IN 1920-21 AND CARRIED 34 AIRCRAFT. HER TWO FUNNELS WERE HINGED SO THAT THEY COULD BE LOWERED WHEN AIRCRAFT WERE "FLYING ON". HER FLIGHT DECK WAS 534 FEET LONG, LESS THAN HALF THE LENGTH OF THE LATEST U.S. CARRIER, U.S.S. ENTERPRISE (1,100 FEET).

JAPANESE CARRIER "AKAGI" (28,100 TONS), ORIGINALLY LAID DOWN AS A 42,000 TONS BATTLECRUISER AND CONVERTED AS A RESULT OF THE WASHINGTON NAVAL TREATY. THE FORE FUNNEL (INTERNALLY DIVIDED INTO FOUR) WAS TRUNKED OUTWARD AND DOWNWARD, WHILE THE SECOND CURVED UPWARD. SHE HAD ACCOMMODATION FOR 50 AIRCRAFT. "AKAGI" WAS SUNK BY THE JAPANESE AFTER BEING BADLY DAMAGED AT MIDWAY...

(BELOW) THE HUGE JAPANESE CARRIER "SHINANO" (71,890 TONS) WAS LAID DOWN AS A BATTLESHIP OF THE "YAMATO" CLASS AND CON-VERTED INTO A CARRIER AFTER THE BATTLE OF MIDWAY. SHE COMMISSIONED ON 19 NOV. 1944 AND WAS SUNK 10 DAYS LATER BY THE U.S. SUBMARINE "ARCHERFISH". HER HUGE FUNNEL SLANTED OUTBOARD AT AN ANGLE OF 26°. SHE HAD STOWAGE FOR ONLY 47 AIRCRAFT, BUT WAS DESIGNED TO PROVIDE A HUGE ARMOURED "EXTRA" FLIGHT DECK FOR OTHER CARRIERS AND FOR SHORE-BASED AIRCRAFT....

J. M. THORNTON

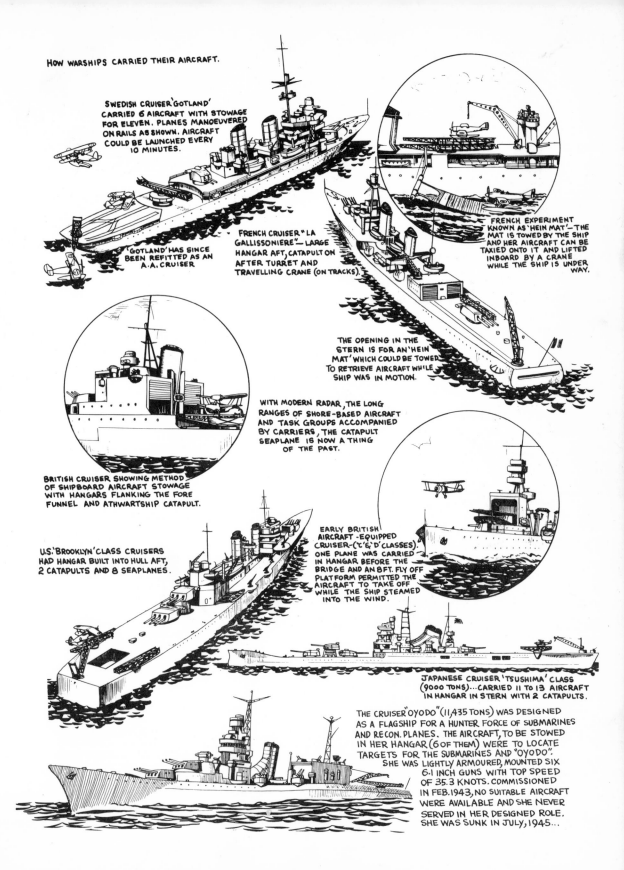

HOW WARSHIPS CARRIED THEIR AIRCRAFT.

SWEDISH CRUISER 'GOTLAND' CARRIED 6 AIRCRAFT WITH STOWAGE FOR ELEVEN. PLANES MANOEUVERED ON RAILS AS SHOWN. AIRCRAFT COULD BE LAUNCHED EVERY 10 MINUTES.

'GOTLAND' HAS SINCE BEEN REFITTED AS AN A.A. CRUISER

FRENCH CRUISER "LA GALLISSONIERE"— LARGE HANGAR AFT, CATAPULT ON AFTER TURRET AND TRAVELLING CRANE (ON TRACKS).

FRENCH EXPERIMENT KNOWN AS 'HEIN MAT'—THE MAT IS TOWED BY THE SHIP AND HER AIRCRAFT CAN BE TAXIED ONTO IT AND LIFTED INBOARD BY A CRANE WHILE THE SHIP IS UNDER WAY.

THE OPENING IN THE STERN IS FOR AN 'HEIN MAT' WHICH COULD BE TOWED TO RETRIEVE AIRCRAFT WHILE SHIP WAS IN MOTION.

WITH MODERN RADAR, THE LONG RANGES OF SHORE-BASED AIRCRAFT AND TASK GROUPS ACCOMPANIED BY CARRIERS, THE CATAPULT SEAPLANE IS NOW A THING OF THE PAST.

BRITISH CRUISER SHOWING METHOD OF SHIPBOARD AIRCRAFT STOWAGE WITH HANGARS FLANKING THE FORE FUNNEL AND ATHWARTSHIP CATAPULT.

U.S. 'BROOKLYN' CLASS CRUISERS HAD HANGAR BUILT INTO HULL AFT, 2 CATAPULTS AND 8 SEAPLANES.

EARLY BRITISH AIRCRAFT-EQUIPPED CRUISER-('C','E','D' CLASSES). ONE PLANE WAS CARRIED IN HANGAR BEFORE THE BRIDGE AND AN 8 FT. FLY OFF PLATFORM PERMITTED THE AIRCRAFT TO TAKE OFF WHILE THE SHIP STEAMED INTO THE WIND.

JAPANESE CRUISER 'TSUSHIMA' CLASS (9000 TONS)...CARRIED 11 TO 13 AIRCRAFT IN HANGAR IN STERN WITH 2 CATAPULTS.

THE CRUISER "OYODO" (11,435 TONS) WAS DESIGNED AS A FLAGSHIP FOR A HUNTER FORCE OF SUBMARINES AND RECON. PLANES. THE AIRCRAFT, TO BE STOWED IN HER HANGAR (6 OF THEM) WERE TO LOCATE TARGETS FOR THE SUBMARINES AND "OYODO". SHE WAS LIGHTLY ARMOURED, MOUNTED SIX 6.1 INCH GUNS WITH TOP SPEED OF 35.3 KNOTS. COMMISSIONED IN FEB.1943, NO SUITABLE AIRCRAFT WERE AVAILABLE AND SHE NEVER SERVED IN HER DESIGNED ROLE. SHE WAS SUNK IN JULY, 1945...

SEAPLANE TENDERS

SEAPLANE TENDERS BECAME AN ESTABLISHED WARSHIP TYPE
BETWEEN THE WARS — PARTICULARLY IN THE U.S. AND
JAPANESE NAVIES WHICH WERE FACED WITH FEW NATURAL
BASES IN THE VASTNESS OF THE PACIFIC OCEAN.

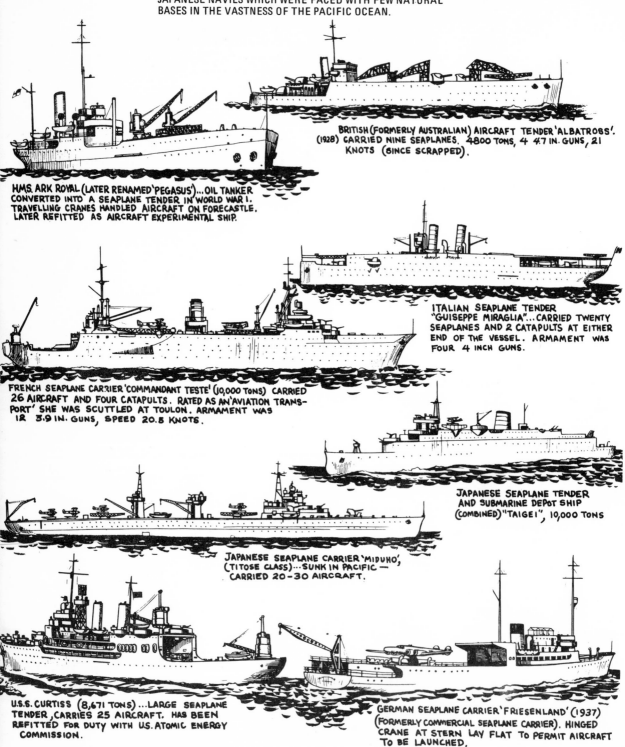

BRITISH (FORMERLY AUSTRALIAN) AIRCRAFT TENDER 'ALBATROSS'.
(1928) CARRIED NINE SEAPLANES. 4800 TONS, 4 4.7 IN. GUNS, 21
KNOTS (SINCE SCRAPPED).

HMS. ARK ROYAL (LATER RENAMED 'PEGASUS')...OIL TANKER
CONVERTED INTO A SEAPLANE TENDER IN WORLD WAR I.
TRAVELLING CRANES HANDLED AIRCRAFT ON FORECASTLE.
LATER REFITTED AS AIRCRAFT EXPERIMENTAL SHIP.

ITALIAN SEAPLANE TENDER
"GUISEPPE MIRAGLIA"...CARRIED TWENTY
SEAPLANES AND 2 CATAPULTS AT EITHER
END OF THE VESSEL. ARMAMENT WAS
FOUR 4 INCH GUNS.

FRENCH SEAPLANE CARRIER 'COMMANDANT TESTE' (10,000 TONS) CARRIED
26 AIRCRAFT AND FOUR CATAPULTS. RATED AS AN 'AVIATION TRANS-
PORT' SHE WAS SCUTTLED AT TOULON. ARMAMENT WAS
12 3.9 IN. GUNS, SPEED 20.5 KNOTS.

JAPANESE SEAPLANE TENDER
AND SUBMARINE DEPOT SHIP
(COMBINED) "TAIGEI", 10,000 TONS

JAPANESE SEAPLANE CARRIER 'MIDUHO',
(TITOSE CLASS)...SUNK IN PACIFIC —
CARRIED 20-30 AIRCRAFT.

U.S.S. CURTISS (8,671 TONS)...LARGE SEAPLANE
TENDER, CARRIES 25 AIRCRAFT. HAS BEEN
REFITTED FOR DUTY WITH U.S. ATOMIC ENERGY
COMMISSION.

GERMAN SEAPLANE CARRIER 'FRIESENLAND' (1937)
(FORMERLY COMMERCIAL SEAPLANE CARRIER). HINGED
CRANE AT STERN LAY FLAT TO PERMIT AIRCRAFT
TO BE LAUNCHED.

J.M.THORNTON

32

FROM THE EARLY YEARS OF THIS CENTURY, NAVAL AIRCRAFT HAVE DEVELOPED FROM KITES AND BALLOONS TO THE PRESENT SUB-SONIC JETS. HERE ARE A FEW THE MORE UNORTHODOX TYPES.

THE R.N.A.S. SOPWITH TRI-PLANE (SINGLE SEATER SCOUT) PRE-DATED THE FAMOUS GERMAN FOKKER TRI-PLANE BY SEVERAL MONTHS. CALLED "THREE DECKERS" BY THEIR NAVAL PILOTS, THEY FLEW OVER THE WESTERN FRONT IN 1917-1918. TOP SPEED WAS 116 M.P.H.

THE BRITISH SUBMARINE SCOUT AIRSHIPS OF WORLD WAR I (ABOVE) WERE VIRTUALLY AEROPLANES WITH GAS BAGS SUBSTITUTED FOR WINGS. A BE·2c FUSELAGE COMPLETE WITH ENGINE WAS SLUNG BENEATH THE ENVELOPE AS A CAR. THEY CRUISED AT 40 M.P.H...

THE "MILES 35" CARRIER FIGHTER (BELOW) NEVER REACHED THE PRODUCTION LINE. WITH TWO PUSHER ENGINES, SHE APPEARED TO BE FLYING BACKWARDS!

THE PONDEROUS FRENCH AMIOT 150-BE SEA-PLANE WAS EMPLOYED AS A TORPEDO BOMBER. WITH A CREW OF 6 AND 3,960 POUNDS OF TORPEDOES AND BOMBS, SHE COULD FLY AT 180 M.P.H. OF PRE-WAR DESIGN, SHE REFLECTED A EUROPEAN TREND TO HEAVY FLOAT PLANES RATHER THAN TO FLYING BOATS..

THE WORLD'S ONLY JET-PROPELLED FLYING-BOAT-FIGHTER WAS BRITAIN'S SAUNDERS-ROE A1. OF POST WAR DESIGN, SHE NEVER REACHED SQUADRON SERVICE ...

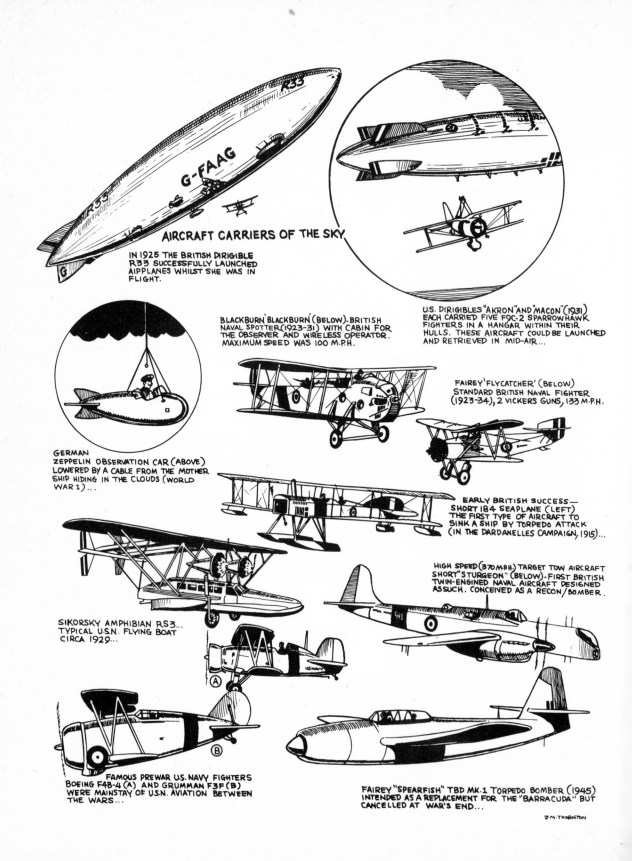

AIRCRAFT CARRIERS OF THE SKY

IN 1925 THE BRITISH DIRIGIBLE R33 SUCCESSFULLY LAUNCHED AIRPLANES WHILST SHE WAS IN FLIGHT.

U.S. DIRIGIBLES "AKRON" AND "MACON" (1931) EACH CARRIED FIVE F9C-2 SPARROWHAWK FIGHTERS IN A HANGAR WITHIN THEIR HULLS. THESE AIRCRAFT COULD BE LAUNCHED AND RETRIEVED IN MID-AIR...

GERMAN ZEPPELIN OBSERVATION CAR (ABOVE) LOWERED BY A CABLE FROM THE MOTHER SHIP HIDING IN THE CLOUDS (WORLD WAR 1)...

BLACKBURN BLACKBURN (BELOW)- BRITISH NAVAL SPOTTER (1923-31) WITH CABIN FOR THE OBSERVER AND WIRELESS OPERATOR. MAXIMUM SPEED WAS 100 M.P.H.

FAIREY 'FLYCATCHER' (BELOW) STANDARD BRITISH NAVAL FIGHTER (1923-34), 2 VICKERS GUNS, 133 M.P.H.

EARLY BRITISH SUCCESS— SHORT 184 SEAPLANE (LEFT) THE FIRST TYPE OF AIRCRAFT TO SINK A SHIP BY TORPEDO ATTACK (IN THE DARDANELLES CAMPAIGN, 1915)...

HIGH SPEED (370 M.P.H.) TARGET TOW AIRCRAFT SHORT "STURGEON" (BELOW)- FIRST BRITISH TWIN-ENGINED NAVAL AIRCRAFT DESIGNED AS SUCH. CONCEIVED AS A RECON/BOMBER.

SIKORSKY AMPHIBIAN RS3... TYPICAL U.S.N. FLYING BOAT CIRCA 1929...

FAMOUS PREWAR U.S. NAVY FIGHTERS BOEING F4B-4 (A) AND GRUMMAN F3F (B) WERE MAINSTAY OF U.S.N. AVIATION BETWEEN THE WARS...

FAIREY "SPEARFISH" TBD MK-1 TORPEDO BOMBER (1945) INTENDED AS A REPLACEMENT FOR THE "BARRACUDA" BUT CANCELLED AT WAR'S END...

J.M. THORNTON

34

"FLIGHTLESS" FLAT TOPS

THE AIRCRAFT CARRIER IS A HIGHLY SPECIALIZED
TYPE OF SHIP.... BUT EVEN THE UNIQUE CON-
FIGURATION OF THE CARRIER HAS UNDERGONE A
VARIETY OF CONVERSIONS FOR USES OTHER
THAN TO OPERATE AIRCRAFT...

(LEFT) H.M.S. UNICORN (1941) WAS DESIGNED AS A
REPAIR/MAINTENANCE CARRIER, BUT DUE TO THE
SHORTAGE OF OPERATIONAL CARRIERS IN 1942,
WAS CONVERTED INTO A COMBATANT UNIT AND
EQUIPPED WITH SWORDFISH AND SEAFIRE AIRCRAFT...

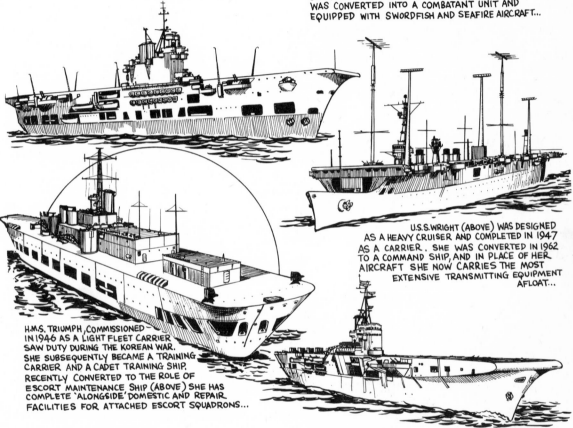

U.S.S. WRIGHT (ABOVE) WAS DESIGNED
AS A HEAVY CRUISER AND COMPLETED IN 1947
AS A CARRIER. SHE WAS CONVERTED IN 1962
TO A COMMAND SHIP, AND IN PLACE OF HER
AIRCRAFT SHE NOW CARRIES THE MOST
EXTENSIVE TRANSMITTING EQUIPMENT
AFLOAT...

H.M.S. TRIUMPH, COMMISSIONED —
IN 1946 AS A LIGHT FLEET CARRIER
SAW DUTY DURING THE KOREAN WAR.
SHE SUBSEQUENTLY BECAME A TRAINING
CARRIER AND A CADET TRAINING SHIP.
RECENTLY CONVERTED TO THE ROLE OF
ESCORT MAINTENANCE SHIP (ABOVE) SHE HAS
COMPLETE 'ALONGSIDE' DOMESTIC AND REPAIR
FACILITIES FOR ATTACHED ESCORT SQUADRONS...

H.M.A.S. SYDNEY (ABOVE) WAS TRANSFERRED
TO AUSTRALIA IN 1949 AS AN OPER-
ATIONAL CARRIER. SHE BECAME A
TRAINING SHIP IN 1955, AND IN 1962
WAS CONVERTED INTO A 'FAST TROOP
TRANSPORT..

H.M. SHIPS 'PIONEER' AND 'PERSEUS' (LEFT)
WERE COMPLETED IN 1945 AS AIRCRAFT
MAINTENANCE SHIPS. THEIR ROLE WAS
TO REPAIR AND FERRY AIRCRAFT FOR
THE OPERATIONAL CARRIERS...

J.M. THORNTON

HELICOPTER 'CARRIERS'

THE GROWING IMPORTANCE OF HELICOPTERS IN THE INVENTORIES OF MOST NAVIES HAS PRODUCED SEVERAL UNIQUE NEW WARSHIP CLASSIFICATIONS TO GET THE "CHOPPERS" TO SEA AS WEAPONS SYSTEMS AND/OR TROOP TRANSPORTERS...

FRENCH HELICOPTER CARRIER "JEANNE D'ARC" (10,000 TONS, 1964) DESIGNED TO CARRY UP TO EIGHT HELICOPTERS. DOUBLES IN PEACE TIME AS A TRAINING SHIP. IN ADDITION SHE IS ARMED WITH FOUR 3.9-INCH GUNS AND A TWIN MASURCA G.M. SYSTEM. SHE IS CAPABLE OF CARRYING A 700-MAN COMMANDO...

H.M.S. 'BLAKE' (BELOW) CONVERTED INTO A HELICOPTER CRUISER FROM A CONVENTIONAL CRUISER (1969) CAN CARRY FOUR A.S.W. OR COMMANDO 'COPTERS IN A LARGE HANGAR ABAFT HER AFTER FUNNEL. TWO 6-INCH AND TWO 3-INCH AUTOMATIC GUNS ARE MOUNTED FORWARD. A SEACAT G.M. SYSTEM COMPLETES THE ARMAMENT....

R.F.A. ENGADINE, BRITISH HELICOPTER SUPPORT SHIP (ABOVE), OF 8,000 TONS, DESIGNED FOR TRAINING 'CHOPPER' CREWS IN ANTI-SUB-MARINE OPERATIONS. AS A ROYAL FLEET AUXILIARY, SHE IS CIVILIAN-MANNED...

NEW ITALIAN HELICOPTER/G.M. CRUISER "VITTORIO VENETO"- 8,850 TONS (32 KNOTS) CAN CARRY UP TO NINE HELICOPTERS IN A HANGAR UNDER HER FLIGHT DECK. ARMAMENT INCLUDES A TERRIER G.M. SYSTEM AND EIGHT 3-INCH GUNS.

RUSSIAN HELICOPTER CARRIER "MOSCOW" (MOSKVA) (1968), DISPLACES 15,000 TONS (STD.) AND HAS ACCOMMODATION FOR ABOUT 30 HELICOPTERS PLUS AN IMPRESSIVE GUIDED MISSILE ARRAY.

MOST OF THESE VESSELS HAVE A CAPABILITY TO OPERATE V.T.O.L. AIRCRAFT NOW BEING DEVELOPED...

J.M. THORNTON

PART THREE

A Half-Century of Cruisers

Cruisers became the successors of the frigates of the sailing fleets and they evolved into classifications. Some of the early armoured and protected cruisers were larger than contemporary battleships and even occupied a position in the line. Others were small, speedy vessels designed for scouting and screening duties. Between the World Wars they became generally grouped into two distinctive types. Those armed with six-inch guns (and lesser calibres) became 'light cruisers', while those armed with heavier guns (usually eight inch) became known as 'heavy cruisers'. The distinction was dictated by the size of the main armament, not the size of the ships themselves.

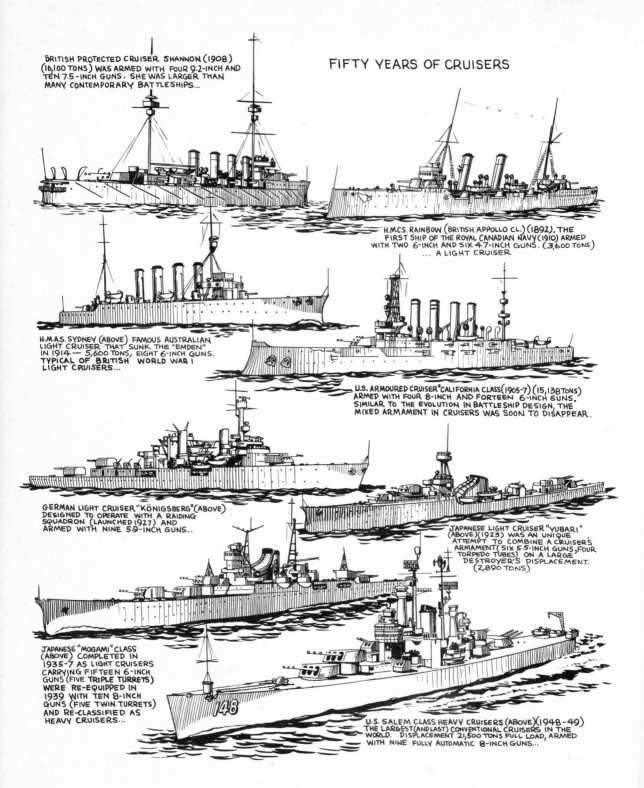

FIFTY YEARS OF CRUISERS

BRITISH PROTECTED CRUISER SHANNON (1908) (16,100 TONS) WAS ARMED WITH FOUR 9.2-INCH AND TEN 7.5-INCH GUNS. SHE WAS LARGER THAN MANY CONTEMPORARY BATTLESHIPS...

H.M.C.S. RAINBOW (BRITISH APPOLLO CL.) (1892), THE FIRST SHIP OF THE ROYAL CANADIAN NAVY (1910) ARMED WITH TWO 6-INCH AND SIX 4.7-INCH GUNS. (3,600 TONS) ... A LIGHT CRUISER

H.M.A.S. SYDNEY (ABOVE) FAMOUS AUSTRALIAN LIGHT CRUISER THAT SUNK THE "EMDEN" IN 1914 — 5,600 TONS, EIGHT 6-INCH GUNS. TYPICAL OF BRITISH WORLD WAR I LIGHT CRUISERS...

U.S. ARMOURED CRUISER "CALIFORNIA CLASS (1905-7) (15,138 TONS) ARMED WITH FOUR 8-INCH AND FORTEEN 6-INCH GUNS. SIMILAR TO THE EVOLUTION IN BATTLESHIP DESIGN, THE MIXED ARMAMENT IN CRUISERS WAS SOON TO DISAPPEAR.

GERMAN LIGHT CRUISER "KÖNIGSBERG" (ABOVE) DESIGNED TO OPERATE WITH A RAIDING SQUADRON (LAUNCHED 1927) AND ARMED WITH NINE 5.9-INCH GUNS..

JAPANESE LIGHT CRUISER "YUBARI" (ABOVE) (1923) WAS AN UNIQUE ATTEMPT TO COMBINE A CRUISER'S ARMAMENT (SIX 5.5-INCH GUNS, FOUR TORPEDO TUBES) ON A LARGE DESTROYER'S DISPLACEMENT. (2,890 TONS)

JAPANESE "MOGAMI" CLASS (ABOVE) COMPLETED IN 1935-7 AS LIGHT CRUISERS CARRYING FIFTEEN 6-INCH GUNS (FIVE TRIPLE TURRETS) WERE RE-EQUIPPED IN 1939 WITH TEN 8-INCH GUNS (FIVE TWIN TURRETS) AND RE-CLASSIFIED AS HEAVY CRUISERS...

U.S. SALEM CLASS HEAVY CRUISERS (ABOVE) (1948-49) THE LARGEST (AND LAST) CONVENTIONAL CRUISERS IN THE WORLD. DISPLACEMENT 21,500 TONS FULL LOAD, ARMED WITH NINE FULLY AUTOMATIC 8-INCH GUNS...

J.M.THORNTON

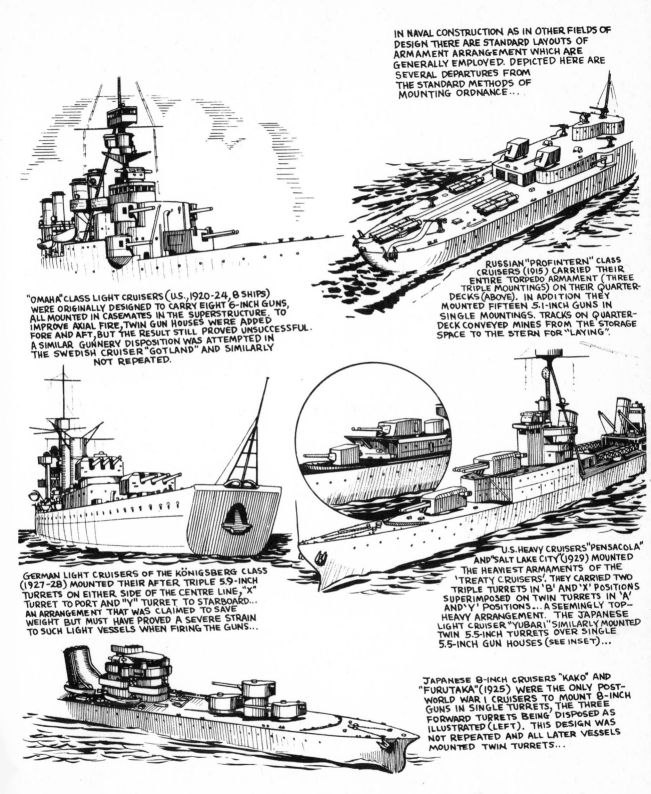

IN NAVAL CONSTRUCTION AS IN OTHER FIELDS OF DESIGN THERE ARE STANDARD LAYOUTS OF ARMAMENT ARRANGEMENT WHICH ARE GENERALLY EMPLOYED. DEPICTED HERE ARE SEVERAL DEPARTURES FROM THE STANDARD METHODS OF MOUNTING ORDNANCE...

"OMAHA" CLASS LIGHT CRUISERS (U.S., 1920-24, 8 SHIPS) WERE ORIGINALLY DESIGNED TO CARRY EIGHT 6-INCH GUNS, ALL MOUNTED IN CASEMATES IN THE SUPERSTRUCTURE. TO IMPROVE AXIAL FIRE, TWIN GUN HOUSES WERE ADDED FORE AND AFT, BUT THE RESULT STILL PROVED UNSUCCESSFUL. A SIMILAR GUNNERY DISPOSITION WAS ATTEMPTED IN THE SWEDISH CRUISER "GOTLAND" AND SIMILARLY NOT REPEATED.

RUSSIAN "PROFINTERN" CLASS CRUISERS (1915) CARRIED THEIR ENTIRE TORPEDO ARMAMENT (THREE TRIPLE MOUNTINGS) ON THEIR QUARTER-DECKS (ABOVE). IN ADDITION THEY MOUNTED FIFTEEN 5.1-INCH GUNS IN SINGLE MOUNTINGS. TRACKS ON QUARTER-DECK CONVEYED MINES FROM THE STORAGE SPACE TO THE STERN FOR "LAYING".

GERMAN LIGHT CRUISERS OF THE KÖNIGSBERG CLASS (1927-28) MOUNTED THEIR AFTER TRIPLE 5.9-INCH TURRETS ON EITHER SIDE OF THE CENTRE LINE, "X" TURRET TO PORT AND "Y" TURRET TO STARBOARD... AN ARRANGEMENT THAT WAS CLAIMED TO SAVE WEIGHT BUT MUST HAVE PROVED A SEVERE STRAIN TO SUCH LIGHT VESSELS WHEN FIRING THE GUNS...

U.S. HEAVY CRUISERS "PENSACOLA" AND "SALT LAKE CITY" (1929) MOUNTED THE HEAVIEST ARMAMENTS OF THE 'TREATY CRUISERS'. THEY CARRIED TWO TRIPLE TURRETS IN 'B' AND 'X' POSITIONS SUPERIMPOSED ON TWIN TURRETS IN 'A' AND 'Y' POSITIONS... A SEEMINGLY TOP-HEAVY ARRANGEMENT. THE JAPANESE LIGHT CRUISER "YUBARI" SIMILARLY MOUNTED TWIN 5.5-INCH TURRETS OVER SINGLE 5.5-INCH GUN HOUSES (SEE INSET)...

JAPANESE 8-INCH CRUISERS "KAKO" AND "FURUTAKA" (1925) WERE THE ONLY POST-WORLD WAR I CRUISERS TO MOUNT 8-INCH GUNS IN SINGLE TURRETS, THE THREE FORWARD TURRETS BEING DISPOSED AS ILLUSTRATED (LEFT). THIS DESIGN WAS NOT REPEATED AND ALL LATER VESSELS MOUNTED TWIN TURRETS...

J. M. THORNTON

THE DOUGHTY "D's"

THE 'D' CLASS WERE THE LAST OF A LONG LINE OF SMALL LIGHT CRUISERS CONCEIVED DURING WORLD WAR I. OF 8 SHIPS COMPLETED (4 WERE CANCELLED) 'DANAE', 'DAUNTLESS', AND 'DRAGON' SAW SERVICE BEFORE THE END OF THE WAR. SMALLER THAN THEIR FOREIGN CONTEMPORARIES, THEY WERE HANDY VESSELS AND GAVE A GOOD ACCOUNT OF THEMSELVES IN WORLD WAR II. ALL EXCEPT 'DESPATCH' WERE FITTED AS FLAGSHIPS. 'DUNEDIN' AND 'DIOMEDE' SERVED IN THE R.N.Z.N. OF 4,850 TONS, THEY MOUNTED SIX 6-INCH GUNS IN SINGLE MOUNTINGS PLUS THREE 4-INCH GUNS AND 12 TORPEDO TUBES. SPEED WAS 29 KNOTS....

H.M.S. DAUNTLESS AS SHE APPEARED IN 1928 WHEN SHE WAS BADLY DAMAGED BY GROUNDING OFF HALIFAX, NOVA SCOTIA. SHE WAS SOLD FOR SCRAP IN 1946...

H.M.S. DAUNTLESS (ABOVE) WITH SEA-PLANE HANGAR BENEATH HER BRIDGE (1918). IT WAS LATER REMOVED.

H.M.S. DUNEDIN (LEFT) AND HER SISTERS 'DELHI', 'DURBAN', 'DESPATCH' AND 'DIOMEDE' WERE PROVIDED WITH TRAWLER BOWS TO IMPROVE THEIR SEA-KEEPING QUALITIES. 'DUNEDIN' WAS SUNK IN THE SOUTH ATLANTIC IN 1941 BY U-124..
'DRAGON' AND 'DANAE' WERE TRANS-FERRED "ON LOAN" TO THE POLISH NAVY DURING WORLD WAR II....

H.M.S. DIOMEDE (RIGHT) DIFFERED FROM HER SISTERS IN THAT HER FORWARD GUN WAS MOUNTED IN A GUN-HOUSE AND THERE WAS NO BLAST SCREEN ON THE SHELTER DECK. NOTE AIRCRAFT PLATFORM ABAFT FUNNELS.

H.M.S. DELHI (LEFT) AS REFITTED AND REARMED LATE IN WORLD WAR II. HER BRIDGE WAS MODERNIZED AND LIGHTER MASTS WERE STEPPED NEGATIVE CONTROL PLATFORMS. SHE WAS RE-ARMED WITH FIVE 5-INCH 38 CAL. (U.S.) GUNS AND NUMEROUS 40 AND 20 MM A.A. GUNS IN U.S.A.
'DELHI' WAS SCRAPPED IN 1948. HER SISTERS 'DRAGON' AND 'DURBAN' WERE EXPENDED AS BLOCK SHIPS FOR THE ARTIFICIAL HARBOUR AT ARROMANCHES, FRANCE IN 1944..

J.M. THORNTON

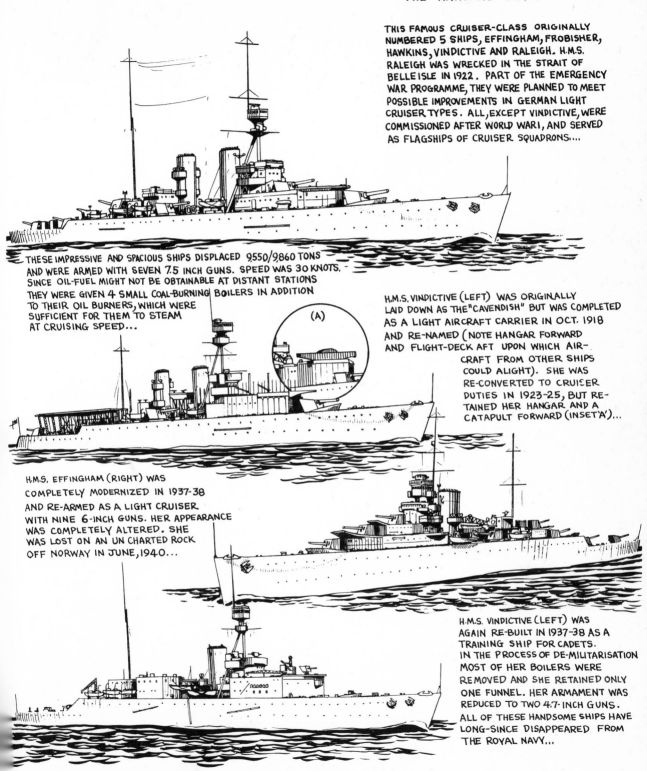

THE "HAWKINS" CLASS

THIS FAMOUS CRUISER-CLASS ORIGINALLY NUMBERED 5 SHIPS, EFFINGHAM, FROBISHER, HAWKINS, VINDICTIVE AND RALEIGH. H.M.S. RALEIGH WAS WRECKED IN THE STRAIT OF BELLE ISLE IN 1922. PART OF THE EMERGENCY WAR PROGRAMME, THEY WERE PLANNED TO MEET POSSIBLE IMPROVEMENTS IN GERMAN LIGHT CRUISER TYPES. ALL, EXCEPT VINDICTIVE, WERE COMMISSIONED AFTER WORLD WAR I, AND SERVED AS FLAGSHIPS OF CRUISER SQUADRONS....

THESE IMPRESSIVE AND SPACIOUS SHIPS DISPLACED 9550/9,860 TONS AND WERE ARMED WITH SEVEN 7.5 INCH GUNS. SPEED WAS 30 KNOTS. SINCE OIL-FUEL MIGHT NOT BE OBTAINABLE AT DISTANT STATIONS THEY WERE GIVEN 4 SMALL COAL-BURNING BOILERS IN ADDITION TO THEIR OIL BURNERS, WHICH WERE SUFFICIENT FOR THEM TO STEAM AT CRUISING SPEED...

(A)

H.M.S. VINDICTIVE (LEFT) WAS ORIGINALLY LAID DOWN AS THE "CAVENDISH" BUT WAS COMPLETED AS A LIGHT AIRCRAFT CARRIER IN OCT. 1918 AND RE-NAMED (NOTE HANGAR FORWARD AND FLIGHT-DECK AFT UPON WHICH AIRCRAFT FROM OTHER SHIPS COULD ALIGHT). SHE WAS RE-CONVERTED TO CRUISER DUTIES IN 1923-25, BUT RETAINED HER HANGAR AND A CATAPULT FORWARD (INSET 'A')...

H.M.S. EFFINGHAM (RIGHT) WAS COMPLETELY MODERNIZED IN 1937-38 AND RE-ARMED AS A LIGHT CRUISER WITH NINE 6-INCH GUNS. HER APPEARANCE WAS COMPLETELY ALTERED. SHE WAS LOST ON AN UNCHARTED ROCK OFF NORWAY IN JUNE, 1940...

H.M.S. VINDICTIVE (LEFT) WAS AGAIN RE-BUILT IN 1937-38 AS A TRAINING SHIP FOR CADETS. IN THE PROCESS OF DE-MILITARISATION MOST OF HER BOILERS WERE REMOVED AND SHE RETAINED ONLY ONE FUNNEL. HER ARMAMENT WAS REDUCED TO TWO 4.7-INCH GUNS. ALL OF THESE HANDSOME SHIPS HAVE LONG-SINCE DISAPPEARED FROM THE ROYAL NAVY...

J.M. THORNTON

41

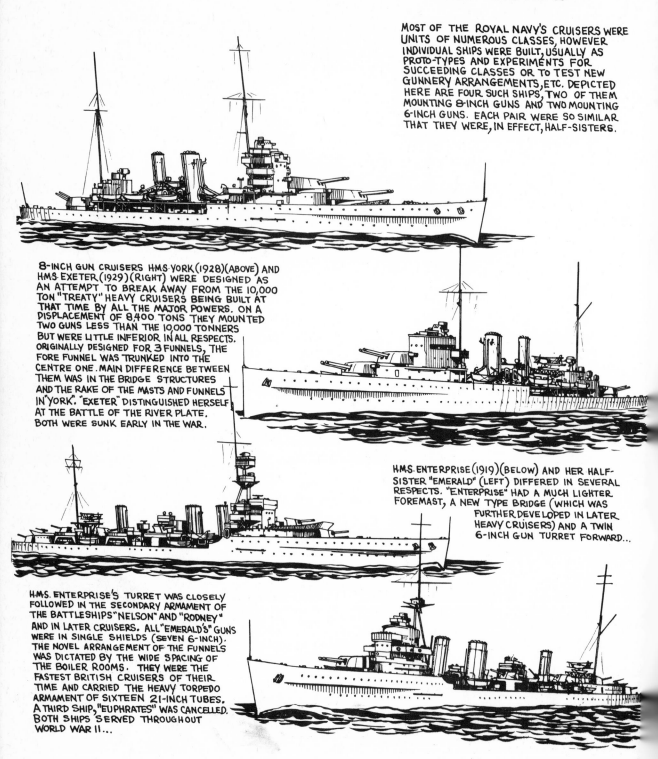

"HALF-SISTERS"

MOST OF THE ROYAL NAVY'S CRUISERS WERE UNITS OF NUMEROUS CLASSES, HOWEVER INDIVIDUAL SHIPS WERE BUILT, USUALLY AS PROTO-TYPES AND EXPERIMENTS FOR SUCCEEDING CLASSES OR TO TEST NEW GUNNERY ARRANGEMENTS, ETC. DEPICTED HERE ARE FOUR SUCH SHIPS, TWO OF THEM MOUNTING 8-INCH GUNS AND TWO MOUNTING 6-INCH GUNS. EACH PAIR WERE SO SIMILAR THAT THEY WERE, IN EFFECT, HALF-SISTERS.

8-INCH GUN CRUISERS H.M.S. YORK (1928) (ABOVE) AND H.M.S. EXETER (1929) (RIGHT) WERE DESIGNED AS AN ATTEMPT TO BREAK AWAY FROM THE 10,000 TON "TREATY" HEAVY CRUISERS BEING BUILT AT THAT TIME BY ALL THE MAJOR POWERS. ON A DISPLACEMENT OF 8,400 TONS THEY MOUNTED TWO GUNS LESS THAN THE 10,000 TONNERS BUT WERE LITTLE INFERIOR IN ALL RESPECTS. ORIGINALLY DESIGNED FOR 3 FUNNELS, THE FORE FUNNEL WAS TRUNKED INTO THE CENTRE ONE. MAIN DIFFERENCE BETWEEN THEM WAS IN THE BRIDGE STRUCTURES AND THE RAKE OF THE MASTS AND FUNNELS IN "YORK". "EXETER" DISTINGUISHED HERSELF AT THE BATTLE OF THE RIVER PLATE. BOTH WERE SUNK EARLY IN THE WAR.

H.M.S. ENTERPRISE (1919) (BELOW) AND HER HALF-SISTER "EMERALD" (LEFT) DIFFERED IN SEVERAL RESPECTS. "ENTERPRISE" HAD A MUCH LIGHTER FOREMAST, A NEW TYPE BRIDGE (WHICH WAS FURTHER DEVELOPED IN LATER HEAVY CRUISERS) AND A TWIN 6-INCH GUN TURRET FORWARD...

H.M.S. ENTERPRISE'S TURRET WAS CLOSELY FOLLOWED IN THE SECONDARY ARMAMENT OF THE BATTLESHIPS "NELSON" AND "RODNEY" AND IN LATER CRUISERS. ALL "EMERALD'S" GUNS WERE IN SINGLE SHIELDS (SEVEN 6-INCH). THE NOVEL ARRANGEMENT OF THE FUNNELS WAS DICTATED BY THE WIDE SPACING OF THE BOILER ROOMS. THEY WERE THE FASTEST BRITISH CRUISERS OF THEIR TIME AND CARRIED THE HEAVY TORPEDO ARMAMENT OF SIXTEEN 21-INCH TUBES. A THIRD SHIP, "EUPHRATES" WAS CANCELLED. BOTH SHIPS SERVED THROUGHOUT WORLD WAR II...

J.M. THORNTON

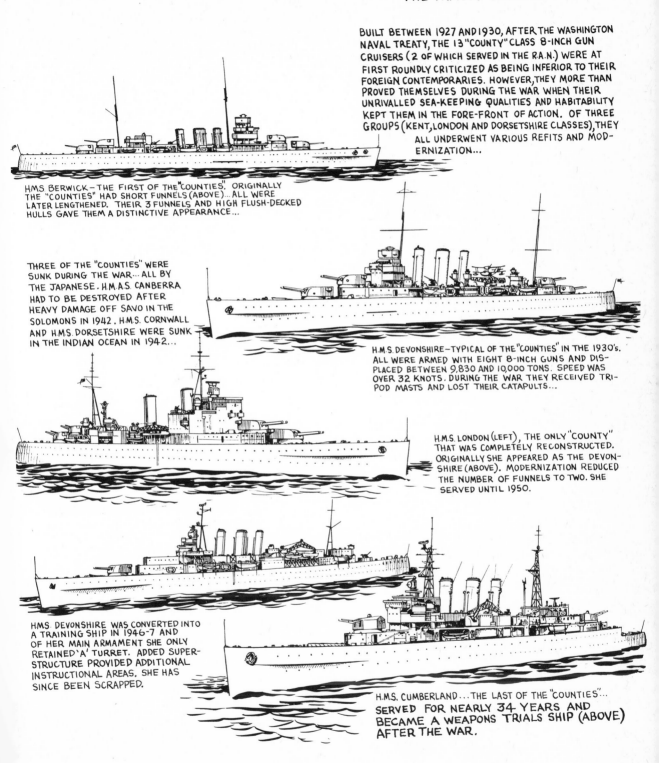

THE FAMOUS "COUNTIES"

BUILT BETWEEN 1927 AND 1930, AFTER THE WASHINGTON NAVAL TREATY, THE 13 "COUNTY" CLASS 8-INCH GUN CRUISERS (2 OF WHICH SERVED IN THE R.A.N.) WERE AT FIRST ROUNDLY CRITICIZED AS BEING INFERIOR TO THEIR FOREIGN CONTEMPORARIES. HOWEVER, THEY MORE THAN PROVED THEMSELVES DURING THE WAR WHEN THEIR UNRIVALLED SEA-KEEPING QUALITIES AND HABITABILITY KEPT THEM IN THE FORE-FRONT OF ACTION. OF THREE GROUPS (KENT, LONDON AND DORSETSHIRE CLASSES), THEY ALL UNDERWENT VARIOUS REFITS AND MODERNIZATION...

H.M.S. BERWICK—THE FIRST OF THE "COUNTIES", ORIGINALLY THE "COUNTIES" HAD SHORT FUNNELS (ABOVE)... ALL WERE LATER LENGTHENED. THEIR 3 FUNNELS AND HIGH FLUSH-DECKED HULLS GAVE THEM A DISTINCTIVE APPEARANCE...

THREE OF THE "COUNTIES" WERE SUNK DURING THE WAR... ALL BY THE JAPANESE. H.M.A.S. CANBERRA HAD TO BE DESTROYED AFTER HEAVY DAMAGE OFF SAVO IN THE SOLOMONS IN 1942. H.M.S. CORNWALL AND H.M.S. DORSETSHIRE WERE SUNK IN THE INDIAN OCEAN IN 1942...

H.M.S. DEVONSHIRE—TYPICAL OF THE "COUNTIES" IN THE 1930's. ALL WERE ARMED WITH EIGHT 8-INCH GUNS AND DISPLACED BETWEEN 9,830 AND 10,000 TONS. SPEED WAS OVER 32 KNOTS. DURING THE WAR THEY RECEIVED TRIPOD MASTS AND LOST THEIR CATAPULTS...

H.M.S. LONDON (LEFT), THE ONLY "COUNTY" THAT WAS COMPLETELY RECONSTRUCTED. ORIGINALLY SHE APPEARED AS THE DEVONSHIRE (ABOVE). MODERNIZATION REDUCED THE NUMBER OF FUNNELS TO TWO. SHE SERVED UNTIL 1950.

H.M.S. DEVONSHIRE WAS CONVERTED INTO A TRAINING SHIP IN 1946-7 AND OF HER MAIN ARMAMENT SHE ONLY RETAINED 'A' TURRET. ADDED SUPERSTRUCTURE PROVIDED ADDITIONAL INSTRUCTIONAL AREAS. SHE HAS SINCE BEEN SCRAPPED.

H.M.S. CUMBERLAND... THE LAST OF THE "COUNTIES"... SERVED FOR NEARLY 34 YEARS AND BECAME A WEAPONS TRIALS SHIP (ABOVE) AFTER THE WAR.

J.M. THORNTON

PART FOUR

Torpedo Boats and Destroyers

The introduction of the locomotive torpedo in the mid 1870s spawned the concept of the torpedo boat, and for the first time in modern history a class of warships emerged without guns as their main armament. At first the new torpedo boats were considered useful only in coastal waters by minor naval powers, but the new type developed rapidly in size and power and soon threatened the battle fleet. A new type of vessel was devised called 'torpedo boat destroyers' designed to protect the battle line from the dreaded new weapon. In time the torpedo boat and its nemesis the torpedo boat destroyer merged into a single type dubbed simply 'destroyers'. They became well-balanced vessels with a mixed armament of light guns and torpedoes on a light hull capable of high speed. These useful 'greyhounds of the fleet' also became known as the 'workhorses of the fleet', screening heavy ships and performing dozens of scouting, escorting and other duties. By the mid 1960s the conventional destroyer had become a vanishing breed, replaced by highly specialised guided-missile and anti-submarine frigates.

TORPEDOES AND TORPEDO VESSELS

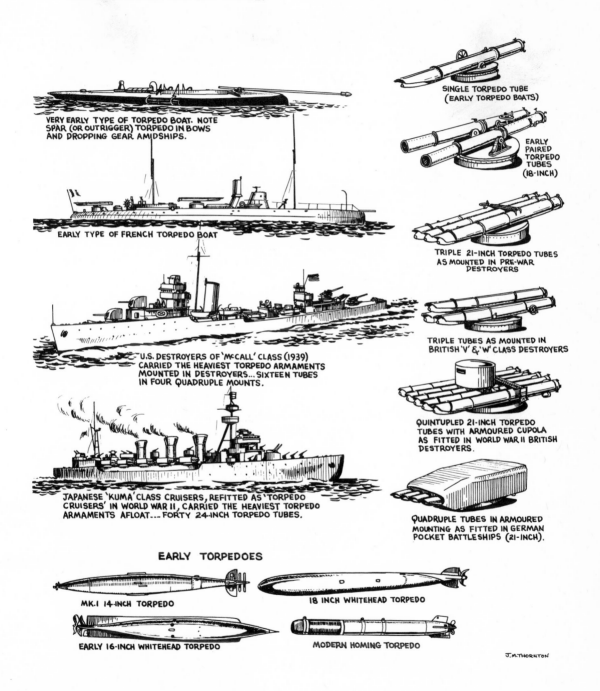

VERY EARLY TYPE OF TORPEDO BOAT. NOTE SPAR (OR OUTRIGGER) TORPEDO IN BOWS AND DROPPING GEAR AMIDSHIPS.

EARLY TYPE OF FRENCH TORPEDO BOAT

U.S. DESTROYERS OF 'McCALL' CLASS (1939) CARRIED THE HEAVIEST TORPEDO ARMAMENTS MOUNTED IN DESTROYERS... SIXTEEN TUBES IN FOUR QUADRUPLE MOUNTS.

JAPANESE 'KUMA' CLASS CRUISERS, REFITTED AS 'TORPEDO CRUISERS' IN WORLD WAR II, CARRIED THE HEAVIEST TORPEDO ARMAMENTS AFLOAT... FORTY 24-INCH TORPEDO TUBES.

SINGLE TORPEDO TUBE (EARLY TORPEDO BOATS)

EARLY PAIRED TORPEDO TUBES (18-INCH)

TRIPLE 21-INCH TORPEDO TUBES AS MOUNTED IN PRE-WAR DESTROYERS

TRIPLE TUBES AS MOUNTED IN BRITISH 'V' & 'W' CLASS DESTROYERS

QUINTUPLED 21-INCH TORPEDO TUBES WITH ARMOURED CUPOLA AS FITTED IN WORLD WAR II BRITISH DESTROYERS.

QUADRUPLE TUBES IN ARMOURED MOUNTING AS FITTED IN GERMAN POCKET BATTLESHIPS (21-INCH).

EARLY TORPEDOES

MK.I 14-INCH TORPEDO

18 INCH WHITEHEAD TORPEDO

EARLY 16-INCH WHITEHEAD TORPEDO

MODERN HOMING TORPEDO

J.M.THORNTON

45

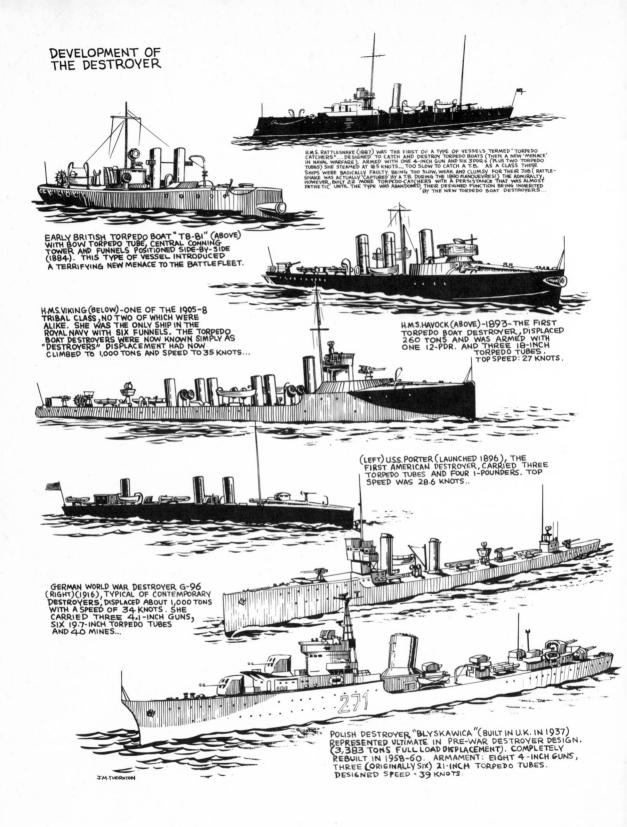

DEVELOPMENT OF THE DESTROYER

H.M.S. RATTLESNAKE (1887) WAS THE FIRST OF A TYPE OF VESSELS TERMED "TORPEDO CATCHERS".... DESIGNED TO CATCH AND DESTROY TORPEDO BOATS (THEN A NEW 'MENACE' IN NAVAL WARFARE). ARMED WITH ONE 4-INCH GUN AND SIX 3PDRS (PLUS TWO TORPEDO TUBES) SHE STEAMED AT 18.5 KNOTS.... TOO SLOW TO CATCH A T.B. AS A CLASS THESE SHIPS WERE BASICALLY FAULTY, BEING TOO SLOW, WEAK AND CLUMSY FOR THEIR JOB (RATTLE-SNAKE WAS ACTUALLY 'CAPTURED' BY A T.B. DURING THE 1890 MANOUEVRES!) THE ADMIRALTY HOWEVER, BUILT 22 MORE TORPEDO-CATCHERS WITH A PERSISTANCE THAT WAS ALMOST PATHETIC UNTIL THE TYPE WAS ABANDONED, THEIR DESIGNED FUNCTION BEING INHERITED BY THE NEW TORPEDO BOAT DESTROYERS...

EARLY BRITISH TORPEDO BOAT "TB-81" (ABOVE) WITH BOW TORPEDO TUBE, CENTRAL CONNING TOWER AND FUNNELS POSITIONED SIDE-BY-SIDE (1884). THIS TYPE OF VESSEL INTRODUCED A TERRIFYING NEW MENACE TO THE BATTLEFLEET.

H.M.S. VIKING (BELOW) — ONE OF THE 1905-8 TRIBAL CLASS, NO TWO OF WHICH WERE ALIKE. SHE WAS THE ONLY SHIP IN THE ROYAL NAVY WITH SIX FUNNELS. THE TORPEDO BOAT DESTROYERS WERE NOW KNOWN SIMPLY AS "DESTROYERS" DISPLACEMENT HAD NOW CLIMBED TO 1,000 TONS AND SPEED TO 35 KNOTS...

H.M.S. HAVOCK (ABOVE) — 1893 — THE FIRST TORPEDO BOAT DESTROYER, DISPLACED 260 TONS AND WAS ARMED WITH ONE 12-PDR. AND THREE 18-INCH TORPEDO TUBES. TOP SPEED: 27 KNOTS.

(LEFT) U.S.S. PORTER (LAUNCHED 1896), THE FIRST AMERICAN DESTROYER, CARRIED THREE TORPEDO TUBES AND FOUR 1-POUNDERS. TOP SPEED WAS 28.6 KNOTS..

GERMAN WORLD WAR DESTROYER G-96 (RIGHT) (1916), TYPICAL OF CONTEMPORARY DESTROYERS, DISPLACED ABOUT 1,000 TONS WITH A SPEED OF 34 KNOTS. SHE CARRIED THREE 4.1-INCH GUNS, SIX 19.7-INCH TORPEDO TUBES AND 40 MINES...

POLISH DESTROYER "BLYSKAWICA" (BUILT IN U.K. IN 1937) REPRESENTED ULTIMATE IN PRE-WAR DESTROYER DESIGN. (3,383 TONS FULL LOAD DISPLACEMENT). COMPLETELY REBUILT IN 1958-60. ARMAMENT: EIGHT 4-INCH GUNS, THREE (ORIGINALLY SIX) 21-INCH TORPEDO TUBES. DESIGNED SPEED = 39 KNOTS.

J·M·THORNTON

DESTROYERS OF THE PAST

DESTROYERS AS WE HAVE KNOWN THEM IN THE PAST ARE FAST BECOMING A DYING BREED. IT IS INTERESTING TO LOOK BACK UPON SHIPS OF THIS FAMOUS TYPE OF OVER 40 YEARS AGO WHEN THEY WERE EVOLVING INTO WHAT, FOR MANY YEARS, WAS THE MOST USEFUL CLASS OF SHIP IN THE NAVIES OF THE WORLD...

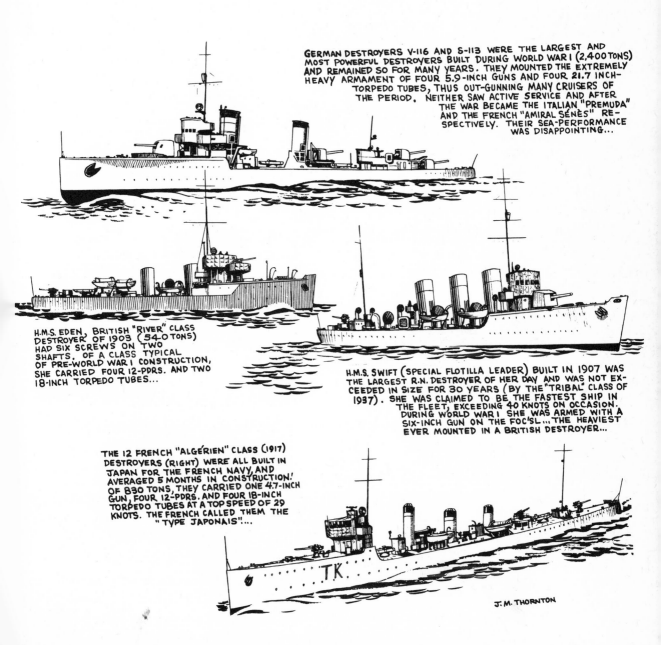

GERMAN DESTROYERS V-116 AND S-113 WERE THE LARGEST AND MOST POWERFUL DESTROYERS BUILT DURING WORLD WAR I (2,400 TONS) AND REMAINED SO FOR MANY YEARS. THEY MOUNTED THE EXTREMELY HEAVY ARMAMENT OF FOUR 5.9-INCH GUNS AND FOUR 21.7 INCH-TORPEDO TUBES, THUS OUT-GUNNING MANY CRUISERS OF THE PERIOD. NEITHER SAW ACTIVE SERVICE AND AFTER THE WAR BECAME THE ITALIAN "PREMUDA" AND THE FRENCH "AMIRAL SÉNÈS" RE-SPECTIVELY. THEIR SEA-PERFORMANCE WAS DISAPPOINTING...

H.M.S. EDEN, BRITISH "RIVER" CLASS DESTROYER OF 1903 (540 TONS) HAD SIX SCREWS ON TWO SHAFTS. OF A CLASS TYPICAL OF PRE-WORLD WAR I CONSTRUCTION, SHE CARRIED FOUR 12-PDRS. AND TWO 18-INCH TORPEDO TUBES...

H.M.S. SWIFT (SPECIAL FLOTILLA LEADER) BUILT IN 1907 WAS THE LARGEST R.N. DESTROYER OF HER DAY AND WAS NOT EX-CEEDED IN SIZE FOR 30 YEARS (BY THE "TRIBAL" CLASS OF 1937). SHE WAS CLAIMED TO BE THE FASTEST SHIP IN THE FLEET, EXCEEDING 40 KNOTS ON OCCASION. DURING WORLD WAR I SHE WAS ARMED WITH A SIX-INCH GUN ON THE FOC'SL... THE HEAVIEST EVER MOUNTED IN A BRITISH DESTROYER...

THE 12 FRENCH "ALGÉRIEN" CLASS (1917) DESTROYERS (RIGHT) WERE ALL BUILT IN JAPAN FOR THE FRENCH NAVY, AND AVERAGED 5 MONTHS IN CONSTRUCTION! OF 830 TONS, THEY CARRIED ONE 4.7-INCH GUN, FOUR 12-PDRS. AND FOUR 18-INCH TORPEDO TUBES AT A TOP SPEED OF 29 KNOTS. THE FRENCH CALLED THEM THE "TYPE JAPONAIS"...

J. M. THORNTON

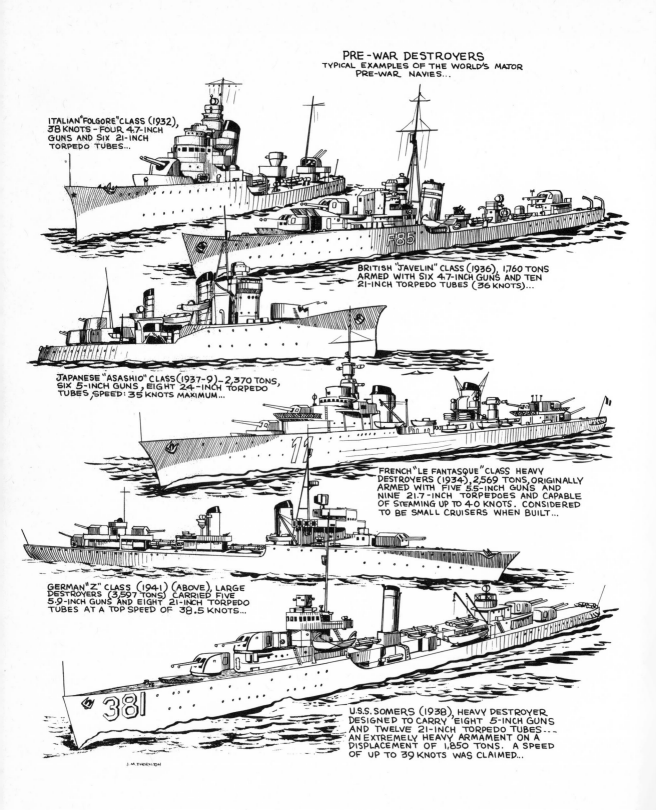

PRE-WAR DESTROYERS
TYPICAL EXAMPLES OF THE WORLD'S MAJOR PRE-WAR NAVIES...

ITALIAN "FOLGORE" CLASS (1932), 38 KNOTS - FOUR 4.7-INCH GUNS AND SIX 21-INCH TORPEDO TUBES...

BRITISH "JAVELIN" CLASS (1936), 1,760 TONS ARMED WITH SIX 4.7-INCH GUNS AND TEN 21-INCH TORPEDO TUBES (36 KNOTS)...

JAPANESE "ASASHIO" CLASS (1937-9) - 2,370 TONS, SIX 5-INCH GUNS, EIGHT 24-INCH TORPEDO TUBES, SPEED: 35 KNOTS MAXIMUM...

FRENCH "LE FANTASQUE" CLASS HEAVY DESTROYERS (1934), 2,569 TONS, ORIGINALLY ARMED WITH FIVE 5.5-INCH GUNS AND NINE 21.7-INCH TORPEDOES AND CAPABLE OF STEAMING UP TO 40 KNOTS. CONSIDERED TO BE SMALL CRUISERS WHEN BUILT...

GERMAN "Z" CLASS (1941) (ABOVE), LARGE DESTROYERS (3,597 TONS) CARRIED FIVE 5.9-INCH GUNS AND EIGHT 21-INCH TORPEDO TUBES AT A TOP SPEED OF 38.5 KNOTS...

U.S.S. SOMERS (1938), HEAVY DESTROYER DESIGNED TO CARRY EIGHT 5-INCH GUNS AND TWELVE 21-INCH TORPEDO TUBES... AN EXTREMELY HEAVY ARMAMENT ON A DISPLACEMENT OF 1,850 TONS. A SPEED OF UP TO 39 KNOTS WAS CLAIMED...

J. M. THORNTON

48

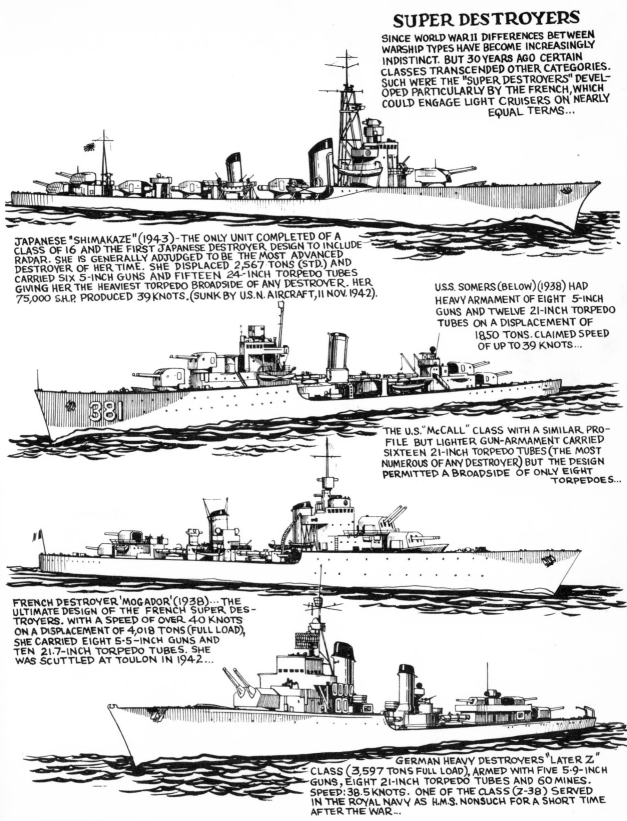

SUPER DESTROYERS

SINCE WORLD WAR II DIFFERENCES BETWEEN
WARSHIP TYPES HAVE BECOME INCREASINGLY
INDISTINCT. BUT 30 YEARS AGO CERTAIN
CLASSES TRANSCENDED OTHER CATEGORIES.
SUCH WERE THE "SUPER DESTROYERS" DEVEL-
OPED PARTICULARLY BY THE FRENCH, WHICH
COULD ENGAGE LIGHT CRUISERS ON NEARLY
EQUAL TERMS...

JAPANESE "SHIMAKAZE" (1943)-THE ONLY UNIT COMPLETED OF A
CLASS OF 16 AND THE FIRST JAPANESE DESTROYER DESIGN TO INCLUDE
RADAR. SHE IS GENERALLY ADJUDGED TO BE THE MOST ADVANCED
DESTROYER OF HER TIME. SHE DISPLACED 2,567 TONS (STD.) AND
CARRIED SIX 5-INCH GUNS AND FIFTEEN 24-INCH TORPEDO TUBES
GIVING HER THE HEAVIEST TORPEDO BROADSIDE OF ANY DESTROYER. HER
75,000 S.H.P. PRODUCED 39 KNOTS. (SUNK BY U.S.N. AIRCRAFT, 11 NOV. 1942).

U.S.S. SOMERS (BELOW) (1938) HAD
HEAVY ARMAMENT OF EIGHT 5-INCH
GUNS AND TWELVE 21-INCH TORPEDO
TUBES ON A DISPLACEMENT OF
1850 TONS. CLAIMED SPEED
OF UP TO 39 KNOTS...

THE U.S. "McCALL" CLASS WITH A SIMILAR PRO-
FILE BUT LIGHTER GUN-ARMAMENT CARRIED
SIXTEEN 21-INCH TORPEDO TUBES (THE MOST
NUMEROUS OF ANY DESTROYER) BUT THE DESIGN
PERMITTED A BROADSIDE OF ONLY EIGHT
TORPEDOES...

FRENCH DESTROYER 'MOGADOR' (1938)... THE
ULTIMATE DESIGN OF THE FRENCH SUPER DES-
TROYERS. WITH A SPEED OF OVER 40 KNOTS
ON A DISPLACEMENT OF 4,018 TONS (FULL LOAD),
SHE CARRIED EIGHT 5·5-INCH GUNS AND
TEN 21.7-INCH TORPEDO TUBES. SHE
WAS SCUTTLED AT TOULON IN 1942...

GERMAN HEAVY DESTROYERS "LATER Z"
CLASS (3,597 TONS FULL LOAD), ARMED WITH FIVE 5·9-INCH
GUNS, EIGHT 21-INCH TORPEDO TUBES AND 60 MINES.
SPEED: 38.5 KNOTS. ONE OF THE CLASS (Z-38) SERVED
IN THE ROYAL NAVY AS H.M.S. NONSUCH FOR A SHORT TIME
AFTER THE WAR...

J.M. THORNTON

THE VENERABLE "V" AND "W"s...

THESE FAMOUS DESTROYERS, OF WHICH THERE WERE OVER 50, WERE DESIGNED IN THE 1914-18 WAR AND SOME SAW SERVICE IN THE FINAL YEAR OF HOSTILITIES. THEY FORMED THE BACKBONE OF THE BRITISH DESTROYER FORCE AFTER THE WAR AND PROVIDED THE BASIC DESIGN FOR SUCCEEDING CLASSES. 40 SURVIVED TO PERFORM VALUABLE WORK IN WORLD WAR II. BETWEEN THEM, THEY SANK 18 U-BOATS. ELEVEN WERE LOST DUE TO ENEMY ACTION...

POPULAR VESSELS IN THEIR DAY, THE "V" AND "W" CLASS DESTROYERS WERE ARMED WITH FOUR 4-INCH GUNS AND SIX TORPEDO TUBES. THEY DISPLACED FROM 1,090 TO 1,100 TONS AND HAD A TOP SPEED OF 34 KNOTS. THEY ALL HAD NAMES STARTING WITH THE LETTERS "V" OR "W".

14 "V" AND "W"s WERE CONVERTED INTO LONG-RANGE ESCORTS (ABOVE). THE FORWARD BOILER ROOM WAS USED FOR EXTRA FUEL STOWAGE AND THEIR SPEED WAS REDUCED TO 24.5 KNOTS. THE TORPEDO TUBES AND HALF THE GUNS WERE REMOVED AND THEY WERE FITTED WITH RADAR AND HF/DF...

A FURTHER 14 OF THESE SHIPS WERE CONVERTED INTO ANTI-AIRCRAFT ESCORTS (KNOWN AS "WAIRS"). THEIR TORPEDO TUBES WERE REMOVED AND THEY WERE ARMED WITH TWO TWIN 4-INCH HIGH-ANGLE GUNS. DISPLACEMENT WAS REDUCED TO 900 TONS...

J.M. THORNTON

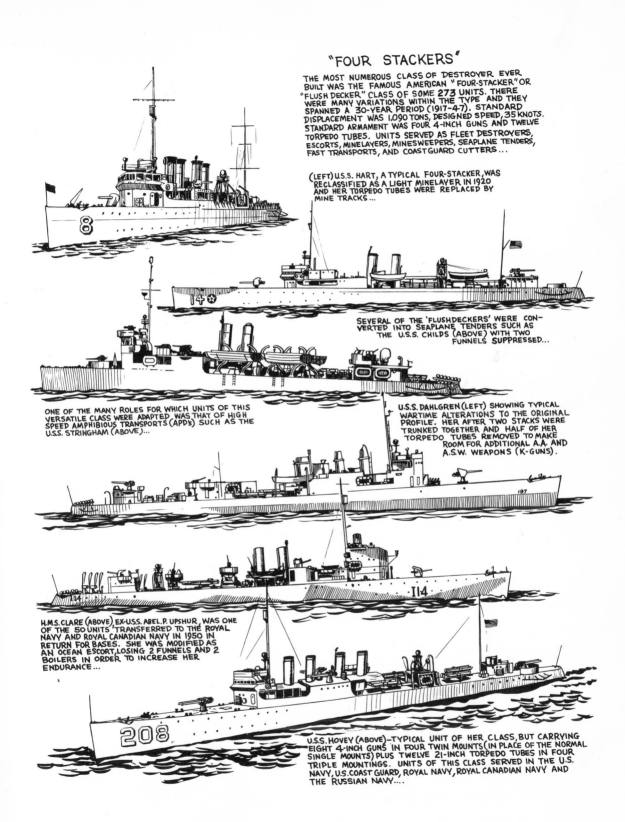

"FOUR STACKERS"

THE MOST NUMEROUS CLASS OF DESTROYER EVER BUILT WAS THE FAMOUS AMERICAN "FOUR-STACKER" OR "FLUSH DECKER" CLASS OF SOME 273 UNITS. THERE WERE MANY VARIATIONS WITHIN THE TYPE AND THEY SPANNED A 30-YEAR PERIOD (1917-47). STANDARD DISPLACEMENT WAS 1,090 TONS, DESIGNED SPEED, 35 KNOTS. STANDARD ARMAMENT WAS FOUR 4-INCH GUNS AND TWELVE TORPEDO TUBES. UNITS SERVED AS FLEET DESTROYERS, ESCORTS, MINELAYERS, MINESWEEPERS, SEAPLANE TENDERS, FAST TRANSPORTS, AND COASTGUARD CUTTERS...

(LEFT) U.S.S. HART, A TYPICAL FOUR-STACKER, WAS RECLASSIFIED AS A LIGHT MINELAYER IN 1920 AND HER TORPEDO TUBES WERE REPLACED BY MINE TRACKS...

SEVERAL OF THE 'FLUSHDECKERS' WERE CONVERTED INTO SEAPLANE TENDERS SUCH AS THE U.S.S. CHILDS (ABOVE) WITH TWO FUNNELS SUPPRESSED...

ONE OF THE MANY ROLES FOR WHICH UNITS OF THIS VERSATILE CLASS WERE ADAPTED WAS THAT OF HIGH SPEED AMPHIBIOUS TRANSPORTS (APD'S) SUCH AS THE U.S.S. STRINGHAM (ABOVE)...

U.S.S. DAHLGREN (LEFT) SHOWING TYPICAL WARTIME ALTERATIONS TO THE ORIGINAL PROFILE. HER AFTER TWO STACKS WERE TRUNKED TOGETHER AND HALF OF HER TORPEDO TUBES REMOVED TO MAKE ROOM FOR ADDITIONAL A.A. AND A.S.W. WEAPONS (K-GUNS).

H.M.S. CLARE (ABOVE), EX-U.S.S. ABEL.P. UPSHUR, WAS ONE OF THE 50 UNITS TRANSFERRED TO THE ROYAL NAVY AND ROYAL CANADIAN NAVY IN 1950 IN RETURN FOR BASES. SHE WAS MODIFIED AS AN OCEAN ESCORT, LOSING 2 FUNNELS AND 2 BOILERS IN ORDER TO INCREASE HER ENDURANCE...

U.S.S. HOVEY (ABOVE) - TYPICAL UNIT OF HER CLASS, BUT CARRYING EIGHT 4-INCH GUNS IN FOUR TWIN MOUNTS (IN PLACE OF THE NORMAL SINGLE MOUNTS) PLUS TWELVE 21-INCH TORPEDO TUBES IN FOUR TRIPLE MOUNTINGS. UNITS OF THIS CLASS SERVED IN THE U.S. NAVY, U.S. COAST GUARD, ROYAL NAVY, ROYAL CANADIAN NAVY AND THE RUSSIAN NAVY....

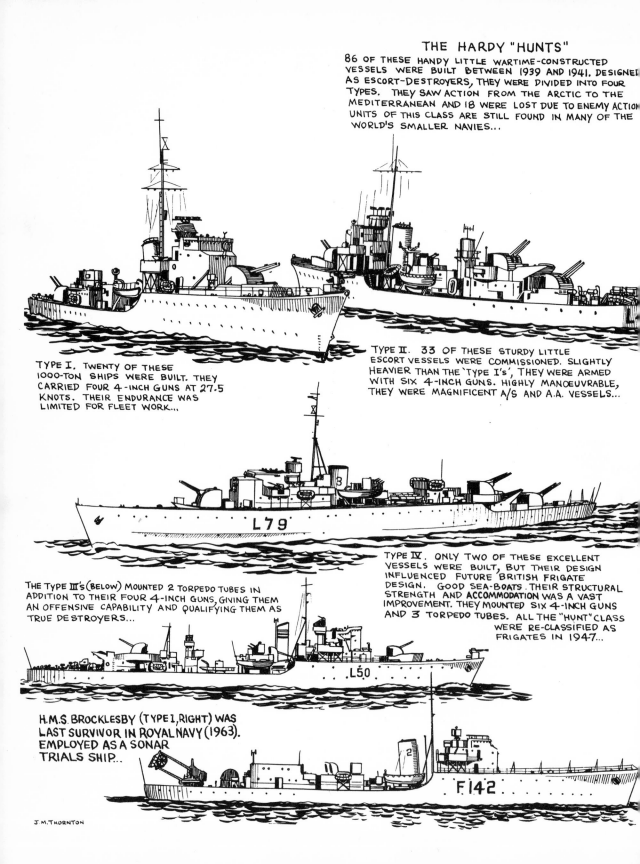

THE HARDY "HUNTS"

86 OF THESE HANDY LITTLE WARTIME-CONSTRUCTED VESSELS WERE BUILT BETWEEN 1939 AND 1941. DESIGNED AS ESCORT-DESTROYERS, THEY WERE DIVIDED INTO FOUR TYPES. THEY SAW ACTION FROM THE ARCTIC TO THE MEDITERRANEAN AND 18 WERE LOST DUE TO ENEMY ACTION UNITS OF THIS CLASS ARE STILL FOUND IN MANY OF THE WORLD'S SMALLER NAVIES...

TYPE I. TWENTY OF THESE 1000-TON SHIPS WERE BUILT. THEY CARRIED FOUR 4-INCH GUNS AT 27.5 KNOTS. THEIR ENDURANCE WAS LIMITED FOR FLEET WORK...

TYPE II. 33 OF THESE STURDY LITTLE ESCORT VESSELS WERE COMMISSIONED. SLIGHTLY HEAVIER THAN THE 'TYPE I's', THEY WERE ARMED WITH SIX 4-INCH GUNS. HIGHLY MANOEUVRABLE, THEY WERE MAGNIFICENT A/S AND A.A. VESSELS...

THE TYPE III's (BELOW) MOUNTED 2 TORPEDO TUBES IN ADDITION TO THEIR FOUR 4-INCH GUNS, GIVING THEM AN OFFENSIVE CAPABILITY AND QUALIFYING THEM AS TRUE DESTROYERS...

TYPE IV. ONLY TWO OF THESE EXCELLENT VESSELS WERE BUILT, BUT THEIR DESIGN INFLUENCED FUTURE BRITISH FRIGATE DESIGN. GOOD SEA-BOATS. THEIR STRUCTURAL STRENGTH AND ACCOMMODATION WAS A VAST IMPROVEMENT. THEY MOUNTED SIX 4-INCH GUNS AND 3 TORPEDO TUBES. ALL THE "HUNT" CLASS WERE RE-CLASSIFIED AS FRIGATES IN 1947...

H.M.S. BROCKLESBY (TYPE 1, RIGHT) WAS LAST SURVIVOR IN ROYAL NAVY (1963). EMPLOYED AS A SONAR TRIALS SHIP...

J.M.THORNTON

PART FIVE

Small Ships

Backing up the glamorous battleships, cruisers with destroyers of the fleet were a myriad of smaller vessels with varying degrees of offensive power. They included gunboats, monitors motor torpedo boats and amphibious craft.

For the period of Pax Britannica gunboats wearing the White Ensign policed the world, but the growing naval strength of Imperial Germany and advancing technology put an end to vessels that 'could neither fight nor run away'.

River gunboats continued to patrol major international rivers and between the wars, and World War II saw the development of high-speed motor gunboats and torpedo boats which had their genesis in the Motor Launches (MLs) of World War I.

The global aspect of World War II forced the rapid evolution of vessels with an amphibious capability, and an entire new spectrum of naval vessels was developed.

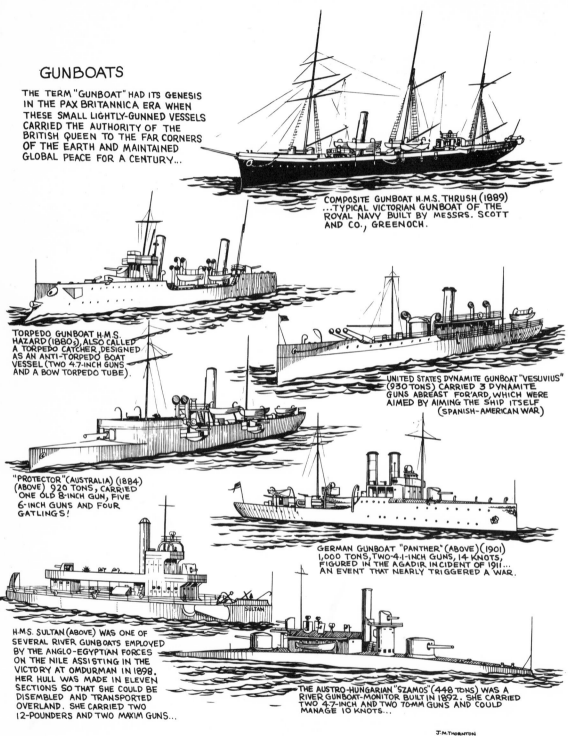

GUNBOATS

THE TERM "GUNBOAT" HAD ITS GENESIS IN THE PAX BRITANNICA ERA WHEN THESE SMALL LIGHTLY-GUNNED VESSELS CARRIED THE AUTHORITY OF THE BRITISH QUEEN TO THE FAR CORNERS OF THE EARTH AND MAINTAINED GLOBAL PEACE FOR A CENTURY...

COMPOSITE GUNBOAT H.M.S. THRUSH (1889) ...TYPICAL VICTORIAN GUNBOAT OF THE ROYAL NAVY BUILT BY MESSRS. SCOTT AND CO., GREENOCH.

TORPEDO GUNBOAT H.M.S. HAZARD (1880s), ALSO CALLED A TORPEDO CATCHER, DESIGNED AS AN ANTI-TORPEDO BOAT VESSEL (TWO 4.7-INCH GUNS AND A BOW TORPEDO TUBE).

UNITED STATES DYNAMITE GUNBOAT "VESUVIUS" (930 TONS) CARRIED 3 DYNAMITE GUNS ABREAST FOR'ARD, WHICH WERE AIMED BY AIMING THE SHIP ITSELF (SPANISH-AMERICAN WAR)

"PROTECTOR" (AUSTRALIA) (1884) (ABOVE) 920 TONS, CARRIED ONE OLD 8-INCH GUN, FIVE 6-INCH GUNS AND FOUR GATLINGS!

GERMAN GUNBOAT "PANTHER" (ABOVE) (1901) 1,000 TONS, TWO-4·1-INCH GUNS, 14 KNOTS, FIGURED IN THE AGADIR INCIDENT OF 1911... AN EVENT THAT NEARLY TRIGGERED A WAR.

H.M.S. SULTAN (ABOVE) WAS ONE OF SEVERAL RIVER GUNBOATS EMPLOYED BY THE ANGLO-EGYPTIAN FORCES ON THE NILE ASSISTING IN THE VICTORY AT OMDURMAN IN 1898. HER HULL WAS MADE IN ELEVEN SECTIONS SO THAT SHE COULD BE DISEMBLED AND TRANSPORTED OVERLAND. SHE CARRIED TWO 12-POUNDERS AND TWO MAXIM GUNS...

THE AUSTRO-HUNGARIAN "SZAMOS" (448 TONS) WAS A RIVER GUNBOAT-MONITOR BUILT IN 1892. SHE CARRIED TWO 4·7-INCH AND TWO 70-MM GUNS AND COULD MANAGE 10 KNOTS...

J.M.THORNTON

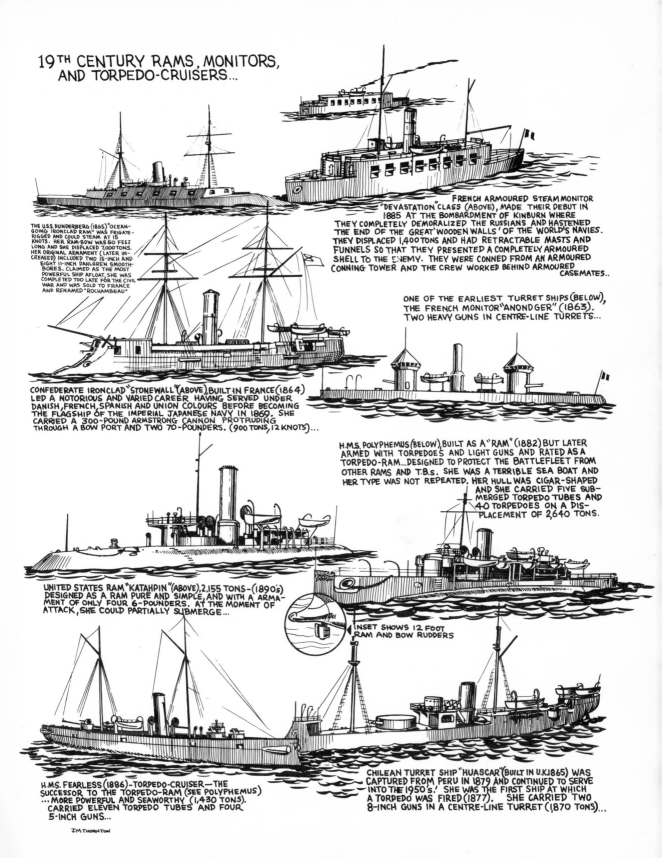

19TH CENTURY RAMS, MONITORS, AND TORPEDO-CRUISERS...

FRENCH ARMOURED STEAM MONITOR "DEVASTATION" CLASS (ABOVE), MADE THEIR DEBUT IN 1885 AT THE BOMBARDMENT OF KINBURN WHERE THEY COMPLETELY DEMORALIZED THE RUSSIANS AND HASTENED THE END OF THE GREAT "WOODEN WALLS" OF THE WORLD'S NAVIES. THEY DISPLACED 1,400 TONS AND HAD RETRACTABLE MASTS AND FUNNELS SO THAT THEY PRESENTED A COMPLETELY ARMOURED SHELL TO THE ENEMY. THEY WERE CONNED FROM AN ARMOURED CONNING TOWER AND THE CREW WORKED BEHIND ARMOURED CASEMATES..

THE U.S.S. DUNDERBERG (1865) "OCEAN-GOING" IRONCLAD RAM" WAS FRIGATE-RIGGED AND COULD STEAM AT 15 KNOTS. HER RAM-BOW WAS 50 FEET LONG AND SHE DISPLACED 7,000 TONS. HER ORIGINAL ARMAMENT (LATER IN-CREASED) INCLUDED TWO 15-INCH AND EIGHT 11-INCH DAHLGREN SMOOTH-BORES. CLAIMED AS THE MOST POWERFUL SHIP AFLOAT, SHE WAS COMPLETED TOO LATE FOR THE CIVIL WAR, AND WAS SOLD TO FRANCE AND RENAMED "ROCHAMBEAU"

ONE OF THE EARLIEST TURRET SHIPS (BELOW), THE FRENCH MONITOR "ANONDGER" (1863). TWO HEAVY GUNS IN CENTRE-LINE TURRETS...

CONFEDERATE IRONCLAD "STONEWALL" (ABOVE), BUILT IN FRANCE (1864) LED A NOTORIOUS AND VARIED CAREER HAVING SERVED UNDER DANISH, FRENCH, SPANISH AND UNION COLOURS BEFORE BECOMING THE FLAGSHIP OF THE IMPERIAL JAPANESE NAVY IN 1869. SHE CARRIED A 300-POUND ARMSTRONG CANNON PROTRUDING THROUGH A BOW PORT AND TWO 70-POUNDERS. (900 TONS, 12 KNOTS)...

H.M.S. POLYPHEMUS (BELOW), BUILT AS A "RAM" (1882) BUT LATER ARMED WITH TORPEDOES AND LIGHT GUNS AND RATED AS A TORPEDO-RAM...DESIGNED TO PROTECT THE BATTLEFLEET FROM OTHER RAMS AND T.B.s. SHE WAS A TERRIBLE SEA BOAT AND HER TYPE WAS NOT REPEATED. HER HULL WAS CIGAR-SHAPED AND SHE CARRIED FIVE SUB-MERGED TORPEDO TUBES AND 40 TORPEDOES ON A DIS-PLACEMENT OF 2,640 TONS.

UNITED STATES RAM "KATAHPIN" (ABOVE), 2,155 TONS - (1890's) DESIGNED AS A RAM PURE AND SIMPLE, AND WITH A ARMA-MENT OF ONLY FOUR 6-POUNDERS. AT THE MOMENT OF ATTACK, SHE COULD PARTIALLY SUBMERGE...

INSET SHOWS 12 FOOT RAM AND BOW RUDDERS

H.M.S. FEARLESS (1886) - TORPEDO-CRUISER — THE SUCCESSOR TO THE TORPEDO-RAM (SEE POLYPHEMUS) ...MORE POWERFUL AND SEAWORTHY (1,430 TONS). CARRIED ELEVEN TORPEDO TUBES AND FOUR 5-INCH GUNS...

CHILEAN TURRET SHIP "HUASCAR" (BUILT IN U.K.1865) WAS CAPTURED FROM PERU IN 1879 AND CONTINUED TO SERVE INTO THE 1950's! SHE WAS THE FIRST SHIP AT WHICH A TORPEDO WAS FIRED (1877). SHE CARRIED TWO 8-INCH GUNS IN A CENTRE-LINE TURRET (1870 TONS)...

J.M.THORNTON

CHINA GUNBOATS

THERE IS NO MORE ROMANTIC PERIOD OF MODERN NAVAL HISTORY THAN THE ERA OF THE CHINA RIVER GUNBOATS. THESE FLAT-BOTTOMED CRAFT WERE MAINTAINED BY THE PRINCIPAL POWERS FROM 1890-1939 ON THE YANGTZE KIANG AND WEST RIVERS OF CHINA TO PROTECT THEIR NATIONALS AGAINST PIRATES, BANDITS AND WAR LORDS, AND WERE CONSTANTLY ON ACTIVE SERVICE NAVIGATING FOR THOUSANDS OF MILES INTO CENTRAL CHINA....

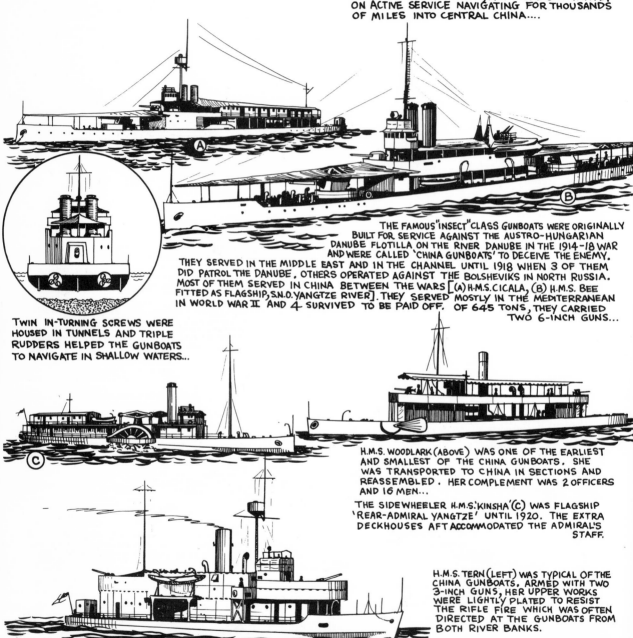

TWIN IN-TURNING SCREWS WERE HOUSED IN TUNNELS AND TRIPLE RUDDERS HELPED THE GUNBOATS TO NAVIGATE IN SHALLOW WATERS...

THE FAMOUS "INSECT" CLASS GUNBOATS WERE ORIGINALLY BUILT FOR SERVICE AGAINST THE AUSTRO-HUNGARIAN DANUBE FLOTILLA ON THE RIVER DANUBE IN THE 1914-18 WAR AND WERE CALLED 'CHINA GUNBOATS' TO DECEIVE THE ENEMY. THEY SERVED IN THE MIDDLE EAST AND IN THE CHANNEL UNTIL 1918 WHEN 3 OF THEM DID PATROL THE DANUBE, OTHERS OPERATED AGAINST THE BOLSHEVIKS IN NORTH RUSSIA. MOST OF THEM SERVED IN CHINA BETWEEN THE WARS [(A) H.M.S. CICALA, (B) H.M.S. BEE FITTED AS FLAGSHIP, S.N.O. YANGTZE RIVER]. THEY SERVED MOSTLY IN THE MEDITERRANEAN IN WORLD WAR II AND 4 SURVIVED TO BE PAID OFF. OF 645 TONS, THEY CARRIED TWO 6-INCH GUNS...

H.M.S. WOODLARK (ABOVE) WAS ONE OF THE EARLIEST AND SMALLEST OF THE CHINA GUNBOATS. SHE WAS TRANSPORTED TO CHINA IN SECTIONS AND REASSEMBLED. HER COMPLEMENT WAS 2 OFFICERS AND 16 MEN...

THE SIDEWHEELER H.M.S. 'KINSHA' (C) WAS FLAGSHIP 'REAR-ADMIRAL YANGTZE' UNTIL 1920. THE EXTRA DECKHOUSES AFT ACCOMMODATED THE ADMIRAL'S STAFF.

H.M.S. TERN (LEFT) WAS TYPICAL OF THE CHINA GUNBOATS, ARMED WITH TWO 3-INCH GUNS, HER UPPER WORKS WERE LIGHTLY PLATED TO RESIST THE RIFLE FIRE WHICH WAS OFTEN DIRECTED AT THE GUNBOATS FROM BOTH RIVER BANKS.

SEVERAL OF THESE GUNBOATS STILL SURVIVE IN THE CHINESE (PEOPLE'S REPUBLIC) NAVY...

J.M.THORNTON

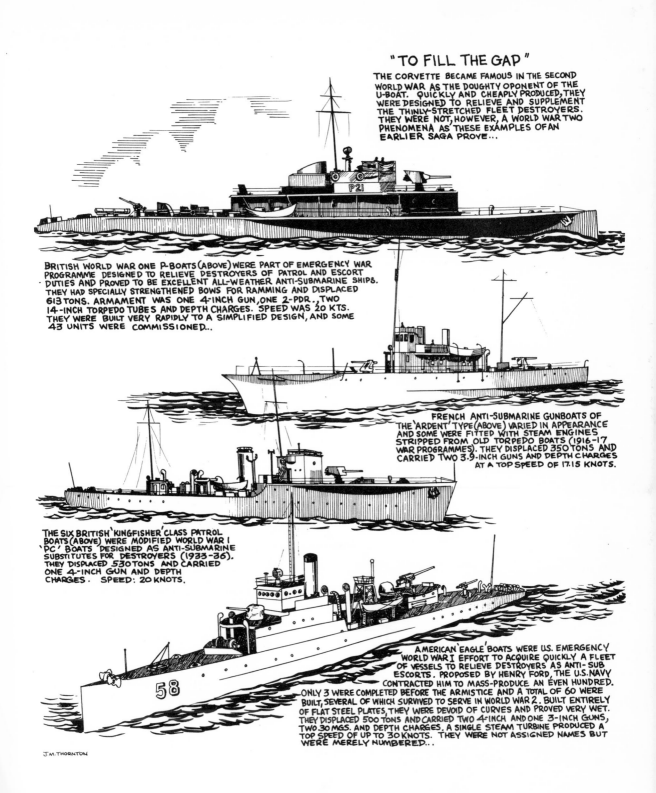

"TO FILL THE GAP"

THE CORVETTE BECAME FAMOUS IN THE SECOND WORLD WAR AS THE DOUGHTY OPONENT OF THE U-BOAT. QUICKLY AND CHEAPLY PRODUCED, THEY WERE DESIGNED TO RELIEVE AND SUPPLEMENT THE THINLY-STRETCHED FLEET DESTROYERS. THEY WERE NOT, HOWEVER, A WORLD WAR TWO PHENOMENA AS THESE EXAMPLES OF AN EARLIER SAGA PROVE...

BRITISH WORLD WAR ONE P-BOATS (ABOVE) WERE PART OF EMERGENCY WAR PROGRAMME DESIGNED TO RELIEVE DESTROYERS OF PATROL AND ESCORT DUTIES AND PROVED TO BE EXCELLENT ALL-WEATHER ANTI-SUBMARINE SHIPS. THEY HAD SPECIALLY STRENGTHENED BOWS FOR RAMMING AND DISPLACED 613 TONS. ARMAMENT WAS ONE 4-INCH GUN, ONE 2-PDR., TWO 14-INCH TORPEDO TUBES AND DEPTH CHARGES. SPEED WAS 20 KTS. THEY WERE BUILT VERY RAPIDLY TO A SIMPLIFIED DESIGN, AND SOME 43 UNITS WERE COMMISSIONED...

FRENCH ANTI-SUBMARINE GUNBOATS OF THE 'ARDENT' TYPE (ABOVE) VARIED IN APPEARANCE AND SOME WERE FITTED WITH STEAM ENGINES STRIPPED FROM OLD TORPEDO BOATS (1916-17 WAR PROGRAMMES). THEY DISPLACED 350 TONS AND CARRIED TWO 3.9-INCH GUNS AND DEPTH CHARGES AT A TOP SPEED OF 17.15 KNOTS.

THE SIX BRITISH 'KINGFISHER' CLASS PATROL BOATS (ABOVE) WERE MODIFIED WORLD WAR I 'PC' BOATS DESIGNED AS ANTI-SUBMARINE SUBSTITUTES FOR DESTROYERS (1933-36). THEY DISPLACED 530 TONS AND CARRIED ONE 4-INCH GUN AND DEPTH CHARGES. SPEED: 20 KNOTS.

AMERICAN 'EAGLE' BOATS WERE U.S. EMERGENCY WORLD WAR I EFFORT TO ACQUIRE QUICKLY A FLEET OF VESSELS TO RELIEVE DESTROYERS AS ANTI-SUB ESCORTS. PROPOSED BY HENRY FORD, THE U.S. NAVY CONTRACTED HIM TO MASS-PRODUCE AN EVEN HUNDRED. ONLY 3 WERE COMPLETED BEFORE THE ARMISTICE AND A TOTAL OF 60 WERE BUILT, SEVERAL OF WHICH SURVIVED TO SERVE IN WORLD WAR 2. BUILT ENTIRELY OF FLAT STEEL PLATES, THEY WERE DEVOID OF CURVES AND PROVED VERY WET. THEY DISPLACED 500 TONS AND CARRIED TWO 4-INCH AND ONE 3-INCH GUNS, TWO .30 MGS. AND DEPTH CHARGES. A SINGLE STEAM TURBINE PRODUCED A TOP SPEED OF UP TO 30 KNOTS. THEY WERE NOT ASSIGNED NAMES BUT WERE MERELY NUMBERED...

J.M.THORNTON

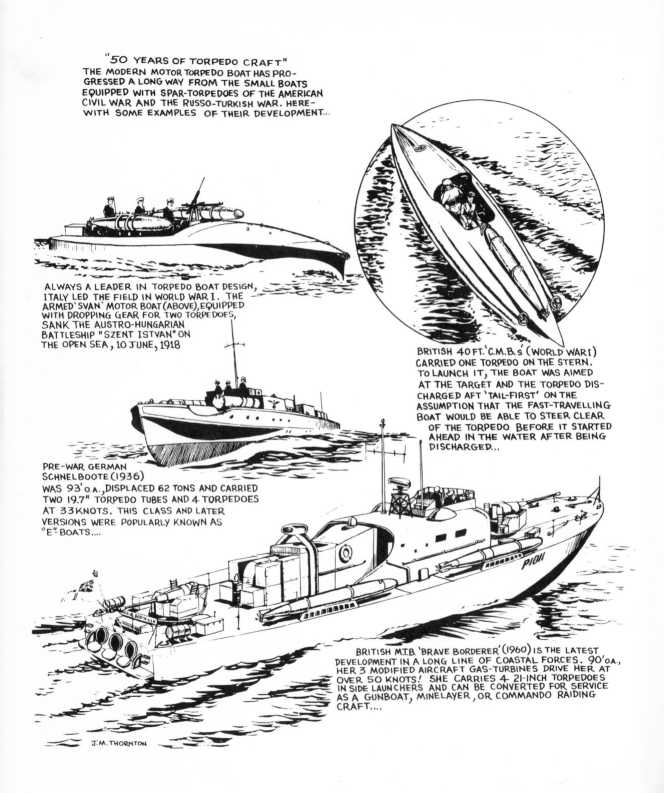

"50 YEARS OF TORPEDO CRAFT"
THE MODERN MOTOR TORPEDO BOAT HAS PRO-
GRESSED A LONG WAY FROM THE SMALL BOATS
EQUIPPED WITH SPAR-TORPEDOES OF THE AMERICAN
CIVIL WAR AND THE RUSSO-TURKISH WAR. HERE-
WITH SOME EXAMPLES OF THEIR DEVELOPMENT...

ALWAYS A LEADER IN TORPEDO BOAT DESIGN,
ITALY LED THE FIELD IN WORLD WAR I. THE
ARMED 'SVAN' MOTOR BOAT (ABOVE), EQUIPPED
WITH DROPPING GEAR FOR TWO TORPEDOES,
SANK THE AUSTRO-HUNGARIAN
BATTLESHIP "SZENT ISTVAN" ON
THE OPEN SEA, 10 JUNE, 1918

BRITISH 40 FT. 'C.M.B.'s' (WORLD WAR I)
CARRIED ONE TORPEDO ON THE STERN.
TO LAUNCH IT, THE BOAT WAS AIMED
AT THE TARGET AND THE TORPEDO DIS-
CHARGED AFT 'TAIL-FIRST' ON THE
ASSUMPTION THAT THE FAST-TRAVELLING
BOAT WOULD BE ABLE TO STEER CLEAR
OF THE TORPEDO BEFORE IT STARTED
AHEAD IN THE WATER AFTER BEING
DISCHARGED...

PRE-WAR GERMAN
SCHNELBOOTE (1936)
WAS 93' O.A., DISPLACED 62 TONS AND CARRIED
TWO 19.7" TORPEDO TUBES AND 4 TORPEDOES
AT 33 KNOTS. THIS CLASS AND LATER
VERSIONS WERE POPULARLY KNOWN AS
"E" BOATS....

BRITISH M.T.B. 'BRAVE BORDERER' (1960) IS THE LATEST
DEVELOPMENT IN A LONG LINE OF COASTAL FORCES. 90' O.A.,
HER 3 MODIFIED AIRCRAFT GAS-TURBINES DRIVE HER AT
OVER 50 KNOTS! SHE CARRIES 4 21-INCH TORPEDOES
IN SIDE LAUNCHERS AND CAN BE CONVERTED FOR SERVICE
AS A GUNBOAT, MINELAYER, OR COMMANDO RAIDING
CRAFT....

J.M. THORNTON

THE UBIQUITOUS FAIRMILES

SOME 750 OF THESE STURDY LITTLE WOODEN VESSELS WERE BUILT DURING WORLD WAR II (102 OF WHICH SERVED IN THE R.C.N.). OF SEVERAL TYPES AND CLASSIFICATIONS, THEY SERVED IN A VARIETY OF ROLES WITH COASTAL FORCES. THEY AVERAGED 65-75 TONS, WITH SPEEDS OF FROM 20 TO 36 KNOTS, DEPENDING ON THE TYPE OF ENGINES FITTED. COMPLEMENTS WERE ABOUT 12 TO 16....

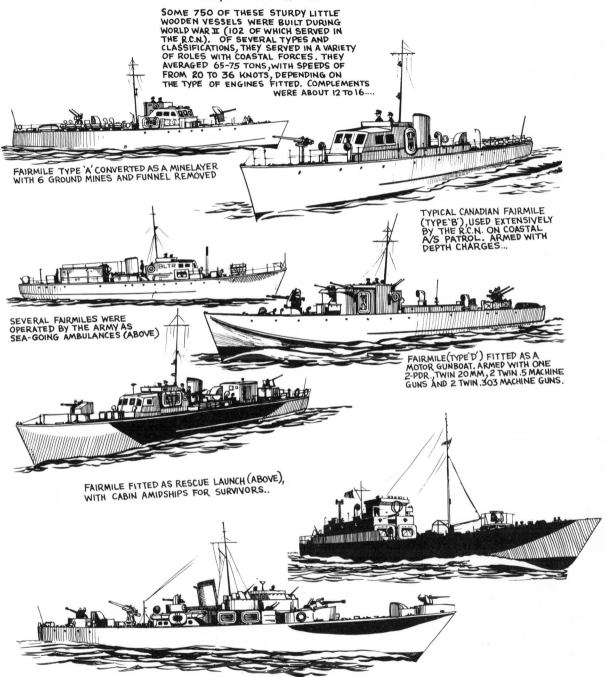

FAIRMILE TYPE 'A' CONVERTED AS A MINELAYER WITH 6 GROUND MINES AND FUNNEL REMOVED

TYPICAL CANADIAN FAIRMILE (TYPE 'B'), USED EXTENSIVELY BY THE R.C.N. ON COASTAL A/S PATROL. ARMED WITH DEPTH CHARGES...

SEVERAL FAIRMILES WERE OPERATED BY THE ARMY AS SEA-GOING AMBULANCES (ABOVE)

FAIRMILE (TYPE 'D') FITTED AS A MOTOR GUNBOAT. ARMED WITH ONE 2-PDR., TWIN 20MM, 2 TWIN .5 MACHINE GUNS AND 2 TWIN .303 MACHINE GUNS.

FAIRMILE FITTED AS RESCUE LAUNCH (ABOVE), WITH CABIN AMIDSHIPS FOR SURVIVORS..

THE 165-TON STEAM GUNBOAT SGB6 MOUNTED A 3-INCH GUN AFT, THREE SINGLE 2-PDRS, FORWARD, AMIDSHIPS AND AFT, A 20-MM BOW-CHASER, 2 SINGLE 20MM IN THE BRIDGE WINGS, TWO TWIN .5 MACHINE GUNS BEFORE THE BRIDGE AND TWO 21-INCH TORPEDO TUBES!

THE MERCANTILE "GAY VIKING" (ABOVE) WAS CONVERTED FROM THE MOTOR TORPEDO BOAT '506' FOR RUNNING THE BLOCKADE THROUGH THE KATTEGAT TO SWEDEN FROM THE U.K. DURING THE WAR. THESE HIGH-SPEED CRAFT CARRIED STRATEGIC CARGOES, AND WERE LIGHTLY ARMED...

EARLY ASSAULT SHIPS

EARLY IN WORLD WAR II, IT BECAME OBVIOUS THAT
SPECIAL VESSELS WOULD HAVE TO BE DEVELOPED AND BUILT
TO FULFIL THE FUNCTIONS OF COMBINED OPERATIONS
EFFICIENTLY. EVENTUALLY THIS FORCE GREW TO BE A
VAST FLEET OF SPECIALIZED SHIPS AND CRAFT. AS A
"STOPGAP" MEASURE, SOME OF THE FIRST SHIPS ASSIGNED
TO DIRECTOR, COMBINED OPERATIONS, WERE CONVERTED
FROM EXISTING VESSELS...

AMONGST THE EARLIEST LANDING SHIPS
(TANK) WERE H.M. SHIPS "BACHEQUERO",
"MISOA" AND "TASAJERO". CONVERTED IN
1941, ORIGINALLY LAKE TANKERS.

MANY LINERS WERE CONVERTED INTO "LANDING
SHIPS, INFANTRY (LARGE), (MEDIUM) AND (SMALL)."
THE THREE FAMOUS "GLEN" SHIPS "GLENGYLE",
"GLENEARD" AND "GLENROY" BECAME LCI(L)s
(ABOVE). THEY COULD ACCOMMODATE 850
TROOPS AND CARRY 12 LCA's AND ONE LCM.

THE FIRST LST'S, BUILT AS SUCH,
WERE H.M.S. BOXER, BRUISER AND
THRUSTER, DESIGNATED LST(1)s.
FROM THEM DEVELOPED THE LST(2)s,
LST(3)s, ETC., ETC., OF WHICH HUNDREDS
WERE EVENTUALLY BUILT IN GREAT
BRITAIN AND U.S.A.

THE ADMIRALTY OILERS "DEWDALE",
"ENNERDALE" AND "DERWENTDALE"
(RIGHT) WERE RIGGED WITH GIANT
GANTRIES AND FITTED TO CARRY
14 LCM(1)s. (LANDING CRAFT, MEDIUM).

J.M. THORNTON

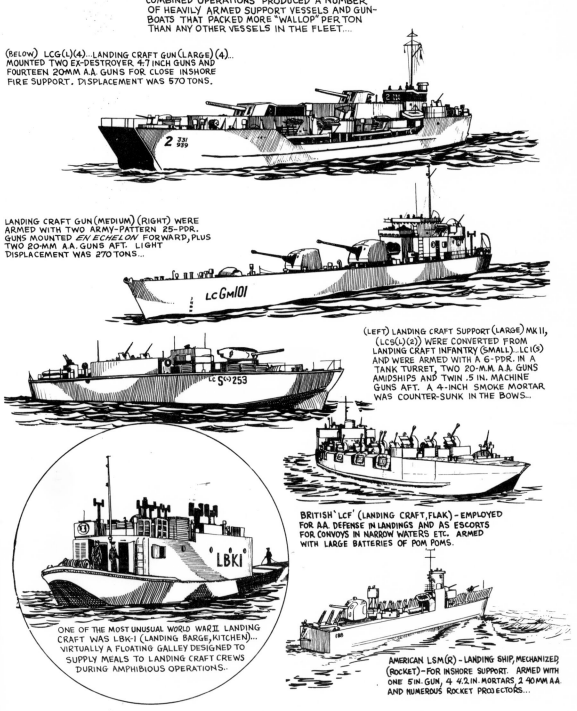

"BIG STINGS IN SMALL PACKAGES"

DURING WORLD WAR II, COASTAL FORCES AND COMBINED OPERATIONS PRODUCED A NUMBER OF HEAVILY ARMED SUPPORT VESSELS AND GUN-BOATS THAT PACKED MORE "WALLOP" PER TON THAN ANY OTHER VESSELS IN THE FLEET....

(BELOW) LCG(L)(4)...LANDING CRAFT GUN (LARGE)(4)... MOUNTED TWO EX-DESTROYER 4.7 INCH GUNS AND FOURTEEN 20MM A.A. GUNS FOR CLOSE INSHORE FIRE SUPPORT. DISPLACEMENT WAS 570 TONS.

LANDING CRAFT GUN (MEDIUM) (RIGHT) WERE ARMED WITH TWO ARMY-PATTERN 25-PDR. GUNS MOUNTED *EN ECHELON* FORWARD, PLUS TWO 20-MM A.A. GUNS AFT. LIGHT DISPLACEMENT WAS 270 TONS...

(LEFT) LANDING CRAFT SUPPORT (LARGE) MK II, (LCS(L)(2)) WERE CONVERTED FROM LANDING CRAFT INFANTRY (SMALL)...LCI(S) AND WERE ARMED WITH A 6-PDR. IN A TANK TURRET, TWO 20-M.M. A.A. GUNS AMIDSHIPS AND TWIN .5 IN. MACHINE GUNS AFT. A 4-INCH SMOKE MORTAR WAS COUNTER-SUNK IN THE BOWS...

BRITISH 'LCF' (LANDING CRAFT, FLAK) - EMPLOYED FOR A.A. DEFENSE IN LANDINGS AND AS ESCORTS FOR CONVOYS IN NARROW WATERS ETC. ARMED WITH LARGE BATTERIES OF POM POMS.

ONE OF THE MOST UNUSUAL WORLD WAR II LANDING CRAFT WAS LBK-I (LANDING BARGE, KITCHEN)... VIRTUALLY A FLOATING GALLEY DESIGNED TO SUPPLY MEALS TO LANDING CRAFT CREWS DURING AMPHIBIOUS OPERATIONS..

AMERICAN LSM(R) - LANDING SHIP, MECHANIZED, (ROCKET) - FOR INSHORE SUPPORT. ARMED WITH ONE 5 IN. GUN, 4 4.2 IN. MORTARS, 2 40MM AA. AND NUMEROUS ROCKET PROJECTORS...

J. M. THORNTON

EARLY MONITORS

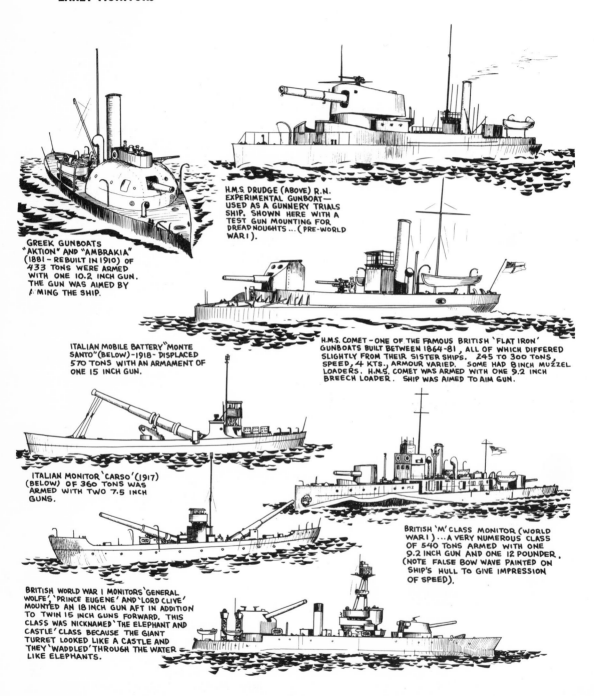

GREEK GUNBOATS
"AKTION" AND "AMBRAKIA"
(1881 - REBUILT IN 1910) OF
433 TONS WERE ARMED
WITH ONE 10.2 INCH GUN.
THE GUN WAS AIMED BY
AIMING THE SHIP.

H.M.S. DRUDGE (ABOVE) R.N.
EXPERIMENTAL GUNBOAT—
USED AS A GUNNERY TRIALS
SHIP. SHOWN HERE WITH A
TEST GUN MOUNTING FOR
DREADNOUGHTS ... (PRE-WORLD
WAR I).

ITALIAN MOBILE BATTERY "MONTE
SANTO" (BELOW) - 1918 - DISPLACED
570 TONS WITH AN ARMAMENT OF
ONE 15 INCH GUN.

H.M.S. COMET - ONE OF THE FAMOUS BRITISH 'FLAT IRON'
GUNBOATS BUILT BETWEEN 1864-81, ALL OF WHICH DIFFERED
SLIGHTLY FROM THEIR SISTER SHIPS. 245 TO 300 TONS,
SPEED, 4 KTS., ARMOUR VARIED. SOME HAD 8 INCH MUZZEL
LOADERS. H.M.S. COMET WAS ARMED WITH ONE 9.2 INCH
BREECH LOADER. SHIP WAS AIMED TO AIM GUN.

ITALIAN MONITOR 'CARSO' (1917)
(BELOW) OF 360 TONS WAS
ARMED WITH TWO 7.5 INCH
GUNS.

BRITISH 'M' CLASS MONITOR (WORLD
WAR I) ... A VERY NUMEROUS CLASS
OF 540 TONS ARMED WITH ONE
9.2 INCH GUN AND ONE 12 POUNDER.
(NOTE FALSE BOW WAVE PAINTED ON
SHIP'S HULL TO GIVE IMPRESSION
OF SPEED).

BRITISH WORLD WAR I MONITORS 'GENERAL
WOLFE', 'PRINCE EUGENE' AND 'LORD CLIVE'
MOUNTED AN 18 INCH GUN AFT IN ADDITION
TO TWIN 15 INCH GUNS FORWARD. THIS
CLASS WAS NICKNAMED 'THE ELEPHANT AND
CASTLE' CLASS BECAUSE THE GIANT
TURRET LOOKED LIKE A CASTLE AND
THEY 'WADDLED' THROUGH THE WATER
LIKE ELEPHANTS.

J.M.THORNTON

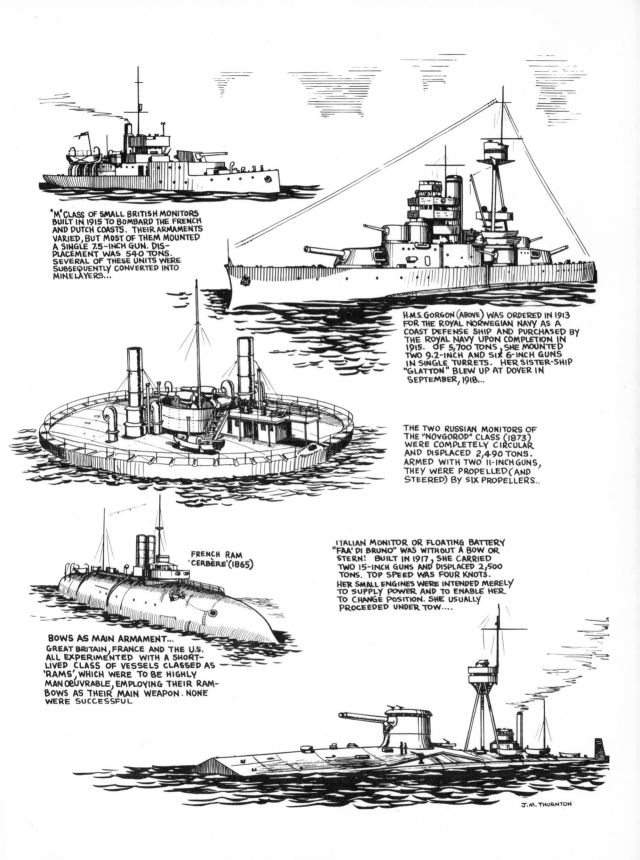

"M" CLASS OF SMALL BRITISH MONITORS
BUILT IN 1915 TO BOMBARD THE FRENCH
AND DUTCH COASTS. THEIR ARMAMENTS
VARIED, BUT MOST OF THEM MOUNTED
A SINGLE 7.5-INCH GUN. DIS-
PLACEMENT WAS 540 TONS.
SEVERAL OF THESE UNITS WERE
SUBSEQUENTLY CONVERTED INTO
MINELAYERS...

H.M.S. GORGON (ABOVE) WAS ORDERED IN 1913
FOR THE ROYAL NORWEGIAN NAVY AS A
COAST DEFENSE SHIP AND PURCHASED BY
THE ROYAL NAVY UPON COMPLETION IN
1915. OF 5,700 TONS, SHE MOUNTED
TWO 9.2-INCH AND SIX 6-INCH GUNS
IN SINGLE TURRETS. HER SISTER-SHIP
"GLATTON" BLEW UP AT DOVER IN
SEPTEMBER, 1918...

THE TWO RUSSIAN MONITORS OF
THE "NOVGOROD" CLASS (1873)
WERE COMPLETELY CIRCULAR
AND DISPLACED 2,490 TONS.
ARMED WITH TWO 11-INCH GUNS,
THEY WERE PROPELLED (AND
STEERED) BY SIX PROPELLERS..

FRENCH RAM
'CERBÈRE' (1865)

ITALIAN MONITOR OR FLOATING BATTERY
"FAA' DI BRUNO" WAS WITHOUT A BOW OR
STERN! BUILT IN 1917, SHE CARRIED
TWO 15-INCH GUNS AND DISPLACED 2,500
TONS. TOP SPEED WAS FOUR KNOTS.
HER SMALL ENGINES WERE INTENDED MERELY
TO SUPPLY POWER AND TO ENABLE HER
TO CHANGE POSITION. SHE USUALLY
PROCEEDED UNDER TOW....

BOWS AS MAIN ARMAMENT...
GREAT BRITAIN, FRANCE AND THE U.S.
ALL EXPERIMENTED WITH A SHORT-
LIVED CLASS OF VESSELS CLASSED AS
'RAMS', WHICH WERE TO BE HIGHLY
MANOEUVRABLE, EMPLOYING THEIR RAM-
BOWS AS THEIR MAIN WEAPON. NONE
WERE SUCCESSFUL

J.M. THORNTON

PART SIX

Submersibles and Submarines

At first considered a cowardly weapon and ignored with contempt by the senior naval officers of the major navies, the submarine evolved rapidly, particularly with the advent of World War I. More than any other weapon it came closer to defeating Great Britain twice in the first half of the twentieth century.

The early 'boats' were more truly described as 'submersibles', or vessels capable of submerging for a short time. This, of course, had tremendous tactical advantages, and by the time that the true submarine, capable of extended under-water operations, was developed in the second half of the twentieth century it had become the most feared weapon in the naval arsenal.

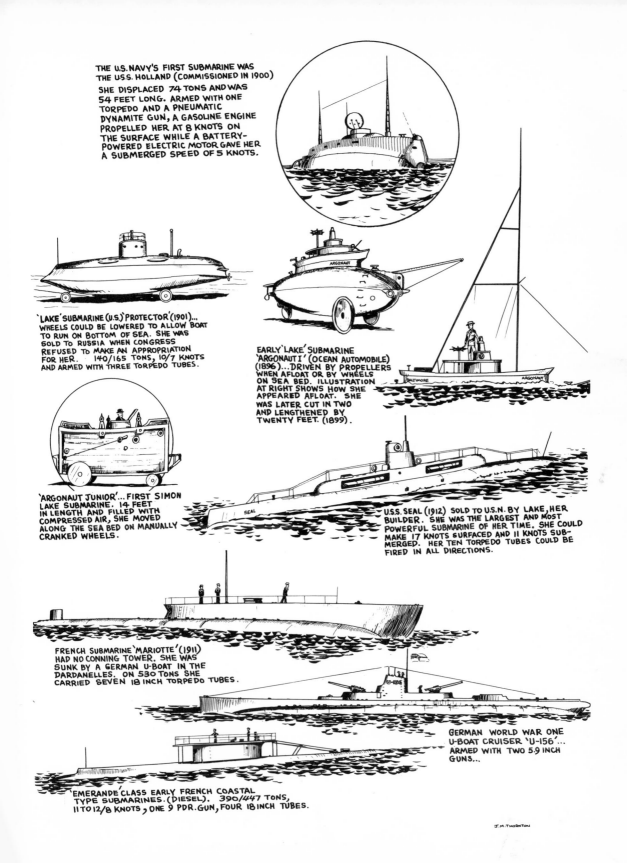

THE U.S.NAVY'S FIRST SUBMARINE WAS THE U.S.S. HOLLAND (COMMISSIONED IN 1900) SHE DISPLACED 74 TONS AND WAS 54 FEET LONG. ARMED WITH ONE TORPEDO AND A PNEUMATIC DYNAMITE GUN, A GASOLINE ENGINE PROPELLED HER AT 8 KNOTS ON THE SURFACE WHILE A BATTERY-POWERED ELECTRIC MOTOR GAVE HER A SUBMERGED SPEED OF 5 KNOTS.

'LAKE' SUBMARINE (U.S.) 'PROTECTOR' (1901)... WHEELS COULD BE LOWERED TO ALLOW BOAT TO RUN ON BOTTOM OF SEA. SHE WAS SOLD TO RUSSIA WHEN CONGRESS REFUSED TO MAKE AN APPROPRIATION FOR HER. 140/165 TONS, 10/7 KNOTS AND ARMED WITH THREE TORPEDO TUBES.

EARLY 'LAKE' SUBMARINE 'ARGONAUT I' (OCEAN AUTOMOBILE) (1896)...DRIVEN BY PROPELLERS WHEN AFLOAT OR BY WHEELS ON SEA BED. ILLUSTRATION AT RIGHT SHOWS HOW SHE APPEARED AFLOAT. SHE WAS LATER CUT IN TWO AND LENGTHENED BY TWENTY FEET. (1899).

'ARGONAUT JUNIOR'... FIRST SIMON LAKE SUBMARINE. 14 FEET IN LENGTH AND FILLED WITH COMPRESSED AIR, SHE MOVED ALONG THE SEA BED ON MANUALLY CRANKED WHEELS.

U.S.S. SEAL (1912) SOLD TO U.S.N. BY LAKE, HER BUILDER. SHE WAS THE LARGEST AND MOST POWERFUL SUBMARINE OF HER TIME. SHE COULD MAKE 17 KNOTS SURFACED AND 11 KNOTS SUB-MERGED. HER TEN TORPEDO TUBES COULD BE FIRED IN ALL DIRECTIONS.

FRENCH SUBMARINE 'MARIOTTE' (1911) HAD NO CONNING TOWER. SHE WAS SUNK BY A GERMAN U-BOAT IN THE DARDANELLES. ON 530 TONS SHE CARRIED SEVEN 18 INCH TORPEDO TUBES.

GERMAN WORLD WAR ONE U-BOAT CRUISER 'U-156'... ARMED WITH TWO 5.9 INCH GUNS...

'EMERANDE' CLASS EARLY FRENCH COASTAL TYPE SUBMARINES. (DIESEL). 390/447 TONS, 11 TO 12/8 KNOTS, ONE 9 PDR.GUN, FOUR 18 INCH TUBES.

J.M.THORNTON

65

EARLY BRITISH SUBMARINES

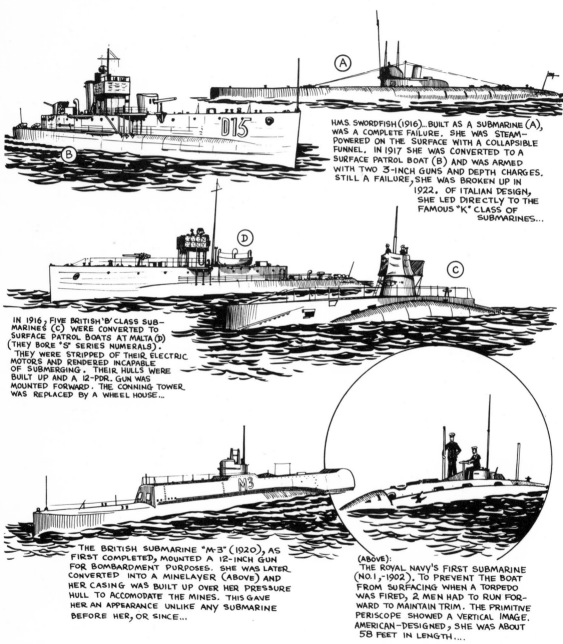

HMS. SWORDFISH (1916)...BUILT AS A SUBMARINE (A), WAS A COMPLETE FAILURE. SHE WAS STEAM-POWERED ON THE SURFACE WITH A COLLAPSIBLE FUNNEL. IN 1917 SHE WAS CONVERTED TO A SURFACE PATROL BOAT (B) AND WAS ARMED WITH TWO 3-INCH GUNS AND DEPTH CHARGES. STILL A FAILURE, SHE WAS BROKEN UP IN 1922. OF ITALIAN DESIGN, SHE LED DIRECTLY TO THE FAMOUS "K" CLASS OF SUBMARINES...

IN 1916, FIVE BRITISH 'B' CLASS SUB-MARINES (C) WERE CONVERTED TO SURFACE PATROL BOATS AT MALTA (D) (THEY BORE 'S' SERIES NUMERALS). THEY WERE STRIPPED OF THEIR ELECTRIC MOTORS AND RENDERED INCAPABLE OF SUBMERGING. THEIR HULLS WERE BUILT UP AND A 12-PDR. GUN WAS MOUNTED FORWARD. THE CONNING TOWER WAS REPLACED BY A WHEEL HOUSE...

THE BRITISH SUBMARINE "M-3" (1920), AS FIRST COMPLETED, MOUNTED A 12-INCH GUN FOR BOMBARDMENT PURPOSES. SHE WAS LATER CONVERTED INTO A MINELAYER (ABOVE) AND HER CASING WAS BUILT UP OVER HER PRESSURE HULL TO ACCOMODATE THE MINES. THIS GAVE HER AN APPEARANCE UNLIKE ANY SUBMARINE BEFORE HER, OR SINCE...

(ABOVE):
THE ROYAL NAVY'S FIRST SUBMARINE (NO.1, -1902). TO PREVENT THE BOAT FROM SURFACING WHEN A TORPEDO WAS FIRED, 2 MEN HAD TO RUN FOR-WARD TO MAINTAIN TRIM. THE PRIMITIVE PERISCOPE SHOWED A VERTICAL IMAGE. AMERICAN-DESIGNED, SHE WAS ABOUT 58 FEET IN LENGTH....

J.M.THORNTON

SUBMARINE GIANTS OF THE PAST

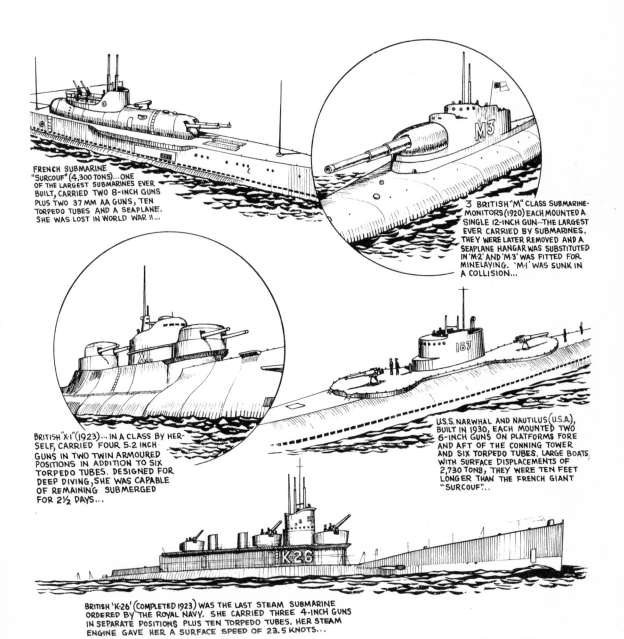

FRENCH SUBMARINE "SURCOUF" (4,300 TONS)... ONE OF THE LARGEST SUBMARINES EVER BUILT, CARRIED TWO 8-INCH GUNS PLUS TWO 37 MM AA GUNS, TEN TORPEDO TUBES AND A SEAPLANE. SHE WAS LOST IN WORLD WAR II...

3 BRITISH "M" CLASS SUBMARINE-MONITORS (1920) EACH MOUNTED A SINGLE 12-INCH GUN...THE LARGEST EVER CARRIED BY SUBMARINES. THEY WERE LATER REMOVED AND A SEAPLANE HANGAR WAS SUBSTITUTED IN 'M-2' AND 'M-3' WAS FITTED FOR MINELAYING. 'M-1' WAS SUNK IN A COLLISION...

BRITISH "X-I" (1923)... IN A CLASS BY HER-SELF, CARRIED FOUR 5.2 INCH GUNS IN TWO TWIN ARMOURED POSITIONS IN ADDITION TO SIX TORPEDO TUBES. DESIGNED FOR DEEP DIVING, SHE WAS CAPABLE OF REMAINING SUBMERGED FOR 2½ DAYS...

U.S.S. NARWHAL AND NAUTILUS (U.S.A.), BUILT IN 1930, EACH MOUNTED TWO 6-INCH GUNS ON PLATFORMS FORE AND AFT OF THE CONNING TOWER AND SIX TORPEDO TUBES. LARGE BOATS, WITH SURFACE DISPLACEMENTS OF 2,730 TONS, THEY WERE TEN FEET LONGER THAN THE FRENCH GIANT "SURCOUF"...

BRITISH 'K-26' (COMPLETED 1923) WAS THE LAST STEAM SUBMARINE ORDERED BY THE ROYAL NAVY. SHE CARRIED THREE 4-INCH GUNS IN SEPARATE POSITIONS PLUS TEN TORPEDO TUBES. HER STEAM ENGINE GAVE HER A SURFACE SPEED OF 23.5 KNOTS...

J.M.THORNTON

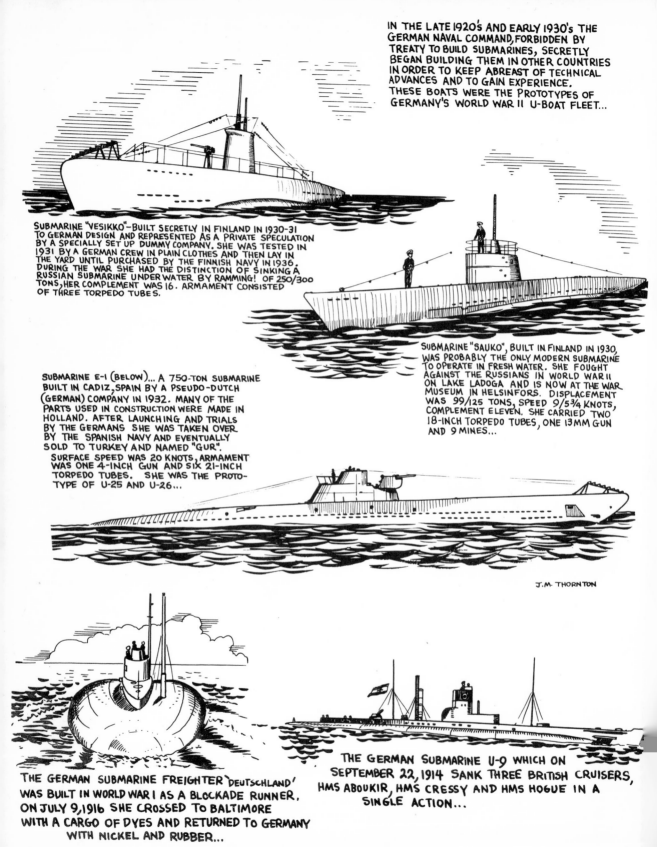

IN THE LATE 1920's AND EARLY 1930's THE GERMAN NAVAL COMMAND, FORBIDDEN BY TREATY TO BUILD SUBMARINES, SECRETLY BEGAN BUILDING THEM IN OTHER COUNTRIES IN ORDER TO KEEP ABREAST OF TECHNICAL ADVANCES AND TO GAIN EXPERIENCE. THESE BOATS WERE THE PROTOTYPES OF GERMANY'S WORLD WAR II U-BOAT FLEET...

SUBMARINE "VESIKKO"—BUILT SECRETLY IN FINLAND IN 1930-31 TO GERMAN DESIGN AND REPRESENTED AS A PRIVATE SPECULATION BY A SPECIALLY SET UP DUMMY COMPANY. SHE WAS TESTED IN 1931 BY A GERMAN CREW IN PLAIN CLOTHES AND THEN LAY IN THE YARD UNTIL PURCHASED BY THE FINNISH NAVY IN 1936. DURING THE WAR SHE HAD THE DISTINCTION OF SINKING A RUSSIAN SUBMARINE UNDER WATER BY RAMMING! OF 250/300 TONS, HER COMPLEMENT WAS 16. ARMAMENT CONSISTED OF THREE TORPEDO TUBES.

SUBMARINE "SAUKO", BUILT IN FINLAND IN 1930, WAS PROBABLY THE ONLY MODERN SUBMARINE TO OPERATE IN FRESH WATER. SHE FOUGHT AGAINST THE RUSSIANS IN WORLD WAR II ON LAKE LADOGA AND IS NOW AT THE WAR MUSEUM IN HELSINFORS. DISPLACEMENT WAS 99/125 TONS, SPEED 9/5¾ KNOTS, COMPLEMENT ELEVEN. SHE CARRIED TWO 18-INCH TORPEDO TUBES, ONE 13MM GUN AND 9 MINES...

SUBMARINE E-1 (BELOW)... A 750-TON SUBMARINE BUILT IN CADIZ, SPAIN BY A PSEUDO-DUTCH (GERMAN) COMPANY IN 1932. MANY OF THE PARTS USED IN CONSTRUCTION WERE MADE IN HOLLAND. AFTER LAUNCHING AND TRIALS BY THE GERMANS SHE WAS TAKEN OVER BY THE SPANISH NAVY AND EVENTUALLY SOLD TO TURKEY AND NAMED "GUR".
SURFACE SPEED WAS 20 KNOTS, ARMAMENT WAS ONE 4-INCH GUN AND SIX 21-INCH TORPEDO TUBES. SHE WAS THE PROTO-TYPE OF U-25 AND U-26...

J.M. THORNTON

THE GERMAN SUBMARINE FREIGHTER 'DEUTSCHLAND' WAS BUILT IN WORLD WAR I AS A BLOCKADE RUNNER. ON JULY 9, 1916 SHE CROSSED TO BALTIMORE WITH A CARGO OF DYES AND RETURNED TO GERMANY WITH NICKEL AND RUBBER...

THE GERMAN SUBMARINE U-9 WHICH ON SEPTEMBER 22, 1914 SANK THREE BRITISH CRUISERS, HMS ABOUKIR, HMS CRESSY AND HMS HOGUE IN A SINGLE ACTION...

J.M.THORNTON

THE MIDGETS AND THE GIANTS

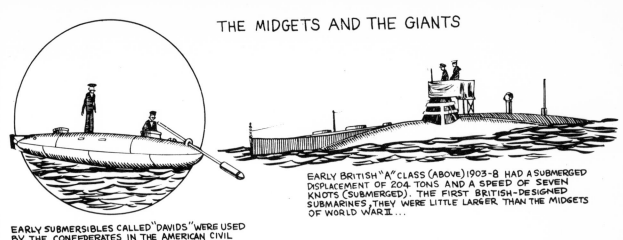

EARLY SUBMERSIBLES CALLED "DAVIDS" WERE USED BY THE CONFEDERATES IN THE AMERICAN CIVIL WAR. ARMED WITH A SPAR TORPEDO, THE 9-MAN CREW WORKED THEM BY HAND. (LATER MODELS USED STEAM).

EARLY BRITISH "A" CLASS (ABOVE) 1903-8 HAD A SUBMERGED DISPLACEMENT OF 204 TONS AND A SPEED OF SEVEN KNOTS (SUBMERGED). THE FIRST BRITISH-DESIGNED SUBMARINES, THEY WERE LITTLE LARGER THAN THE MIDGETS OF WORLD WAR II...

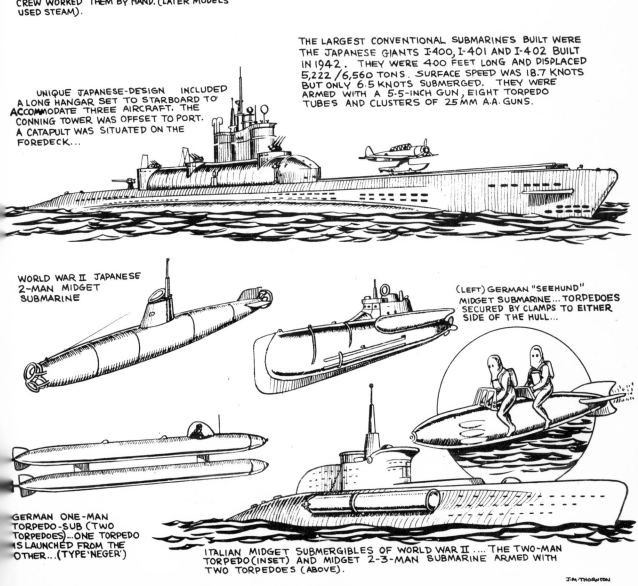

UNIQUE JAPANESE-DESIGN INCLUDED A LONG HANGAR SET TO STARBOARD TO ACCOMMODATE THREE AIRCRAFT. THE CONNING TOWER WAS OFFSET TO PORT. A CATAPULT WAS SITUATED ON THE FOREDECK...

THE LARGEST CONVENTIONAL SUBMARINES BUILT WERE THE JAPANESE GIANTS I-400, I-401 AND I-402 BUILT IN 1942. THEY WERE 400 FEET LONG AND DISPLACED 5,222/6,560 TONS. SURFACE SPEED WAS 18.7 KNOTS BUT ONLY 6.5 KNOTS SUBMERGED. THEY WERE ARMED WITH A 5.5-INCH GUN, EIGHT TORPEDO TUBES AND CLUSTERS OF 25MM A.A. GUNS.

WORLD WAR II JAPANESE 2-MAN MIDGET SUBMARINE

(LEFT) GERMAN "SEEHUND" MIDGET SUBMARINE... TORPEDOES SECURED BY CLAMPS TO EITHER SIDE OF THE HULL...

GERMAN ONE-MAN TORPEDO-SUB (TWO TORPEDOES)...ONE TORPEDO IS LAUNCHED FROM THE OTHER...(TYPE 'NEGER')

ITALIAN MIDGET SUBMERGIBLES OF WORLD WAR II.... THE TWO-MAN TORPEDO (INSET) AND MIDGET 2-3-MAN SUBMARINE ARMED WITH TWO TORPEDOES (ABOVE).

J.M. THORNTON

69

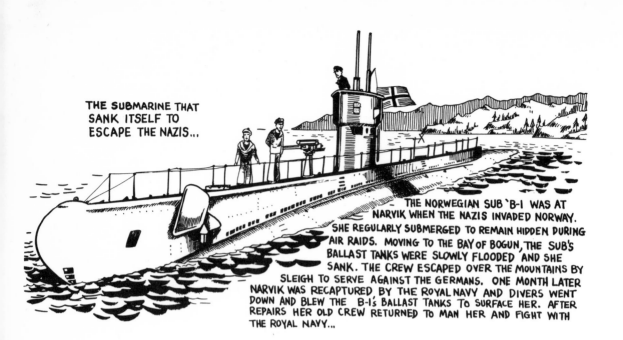

THE SUBMARINE THAT
SANK ITSELF TO
ESCAPE THE NAZIS...

THE NORWEGIAN SUB 'B-1 WAS AT
NARVIK WHEN THE NAZIS INVADED NORWAY.
SHE REGULARLY SUBMERGED TO REMAIN HIDDEN DURING
AIR RAIDS. MOVING TO THE BAY OF BOGUN, THE SUB'S
BALLAST TANKS WERE SLOWLY FLOODED AND SHE
SANK. THE CREW ESCAPED OVER THE MOUNTAINS BY
SLEIGH TO SERVE AGAINST THE GERMANS. ONE MONTH LATER
NARVIK WAS RECAPTURED BY THE ROYAL NAVY AND DIVERS WENT
DOWN AND BLEW THE B-1's BALLAST TANKS TO SURFACE HER. AFTER
REPAIRS HER OLD CREW RETURNED TO MAN HER AND FIGHT WITH
THE ROYAL NAVY...

PART SEVEN

Warships That Might Have Been

The annals of twentieth-century naval construction are studded with the short histories of capital ships that, for one reason or another, never reached their destined element. Treaty limitations, changes of government, enemy action, financial cutbacks, premature obsolescence — all were responsible for the cancellations of major warships, some of which, had they been completed, might well have changed the course of history. Of these great ships that never sailed, some were merely in the projected or appropriated stage when revoked. Others had reached the design step, the building phase, and indeed, the fitting out stage before they were stricken. A few were even eventually commissioned, but not until they had been completely redesigned and rebuilt to serve in roles far removed from the original.

NAVAL DREAMS

H.M.S. INCOMPARABLE – HUGE MOTOR BATTLECRUISER

LORD FISHER, THE FAMOUS AND VISIONARY FIRST SEA LORD WHO INTRODUCED THE
'DREADNOUGHT' AND SUCH FREAKS AS THE 'FURIOUS', 'GLORIOUS' AND 'COURAGEOUS',
ALSO PROPOSED THE ABOVE ENORMOUS OIL-BURNING, SHALLOW DRAUGHT BATTLE-
CRUISER IN 1912.   1,000 FEET LONG, IT WAS TO BE ARMED WITH SIX 20 INCH
GUNS. IT WAS TO BE VERY LIGHTLY BUILT WITH A CENTRAL ARMOURED
CIDATEL 16 INCHES THICK. IT WAS DESIGNED ONLY TO LAST 10 YEARS, FOR HE
REASONED ALL WARSHIPS BECAME OBSOLETE WITHIN THAT TIME. TOP SPEED
WAS TO BE OVER 32 KNOTS AND IT COULD SAIL AROUND
THE WORLD WITHOUT REFUELLING. COFFER DAMS IN ITS
HONEYCOMBED DOUBLE BOTTOM WERE TO BE FILLED WITH CORK.

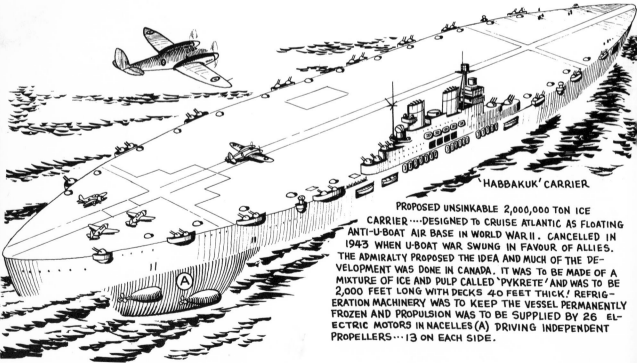

'HABBAKUK' CARRIER

PROPOSED UNSINKABLE 2,000,000 TON ICE
CARRIER ···· DESIGNED TO CRUISE ATLANTIC AS FLOATING
ANTI-U-BOAT AIR BASE IN WORLD WAR II. CANCELLED IN
1943 WHEN U-BOAT WAR SWUNG IN FAVOUR OF ALLIES.
THE ADMIRALTY PROPOSED THE IDEA AND MUCH OF THE DE-
VELOPMENT WAS DONE IN CANADA. IT WAS TO BE MADE OF A
MIXTURE OF ICE AND PULP CALLED 'PYKRETE' AND WAS TO BE
2,000 FEET LONG WITH DECKS 40 FEET THICK! REFRIG-
ERATION MACHINERY WAS TO KEEP THE VESSEL PERMANENTLY
FROZEN AND PROPULSION WAS TO BE SUPPLIED BY 26 EL-
ECTRIC MOTORS IN NACELLES (A) DRIVING INDEPENDENT
PROPELLERS ··· 13 ON EACH SIDE.

J. M. THORNTON

CANCELLED CAPITAL SHIPS

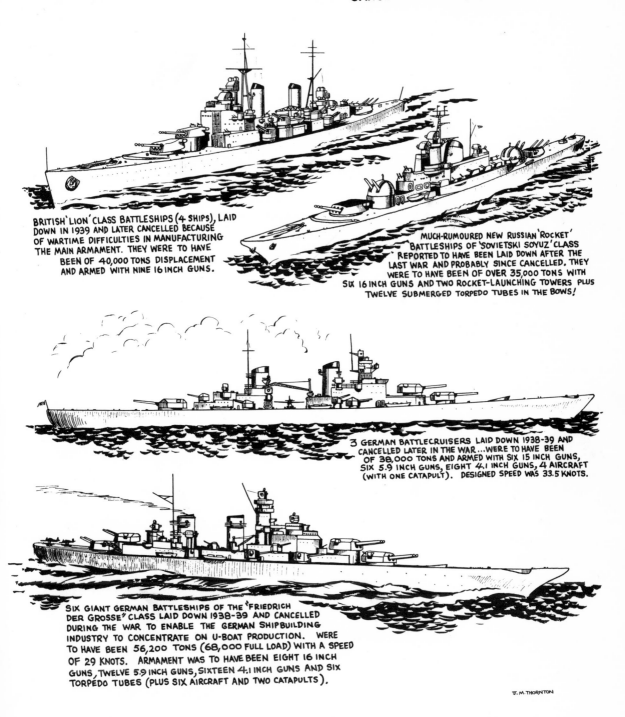

BRITISH 'LION' CLASS BATTLESHIPS (4 SHIPS), LAID DOWN IN 1939 AND LATER CANCELLED BECAUSE OF WARTIME DIFFICULTIES IN MANUFACTURING THE MAIN ARMAMENT. THEY WERE TO HAVE BEEN OF 40,000 TONS DISPLACEMENT AND ARMED WITH NINE 16 INCH GUNS.

MUCH-RUMOURED NEW RUSSIAN 'ROCKET' BATTLESHIPS OF 'SOVIETSKI SOYUZ' CLASS REPORTED TO HAVE BEEN LAID DOWN AFTER THE LAST WAR AND PROBABLY SINCE CANCELLED. THEY WERE TO HAVE BEEN OF OVER 35,000 TONS WITH SIX 16 INCH GUNS AND TWO ROCKET-LAUNCHING TOWERS PLUS TWELVE SUBMERGED TORPEDO TUBES IN THE BOWS!

3 GERMAN BATTLECRUISERS LAID DOWN 1938-39 AND CANCELLED LATER IN THE WAR...WERE TO HAVE BEEN OF 38,000 TONS AND ARMED WITH SIX 15 INCH GUNS, SIX 5.9 INCH GUNS, EIGHT 4.1 INCH GUNS, 4 AIRCRAFT (WITH ONE CATAPULT). DESIGNED SPEED WAS 33.5 KNOTS.

SIX GIANT GERMAN BATTLESHIPS OF THE 'FRIEDRICH DER GROSSE' CLASS LAID DOWN 1938-39 AND CANCELLED DURING THE WAR TO ENABLE THE GERMAN SHIPBUILDING INDUSTRY TO CONCENTRATE ON U-BOAT PRODUCTION. WERE TO HAVE BEEN 56,200 TONS (68,000 FULL LOAD) WITH A SPEED OF 29 KNOTS. ARMAMENT WAS TO HAVE BEEN EIGHT 16 INCH GUNS, TWELVE 5.9 INCH GUNS, SIXTEEN 4.1 INCH GUNS AND SIX TORPEDO TUBES (PLUS SIX AIRCRAFT AND TWO CATAPULTS).

J. M. THORNTON

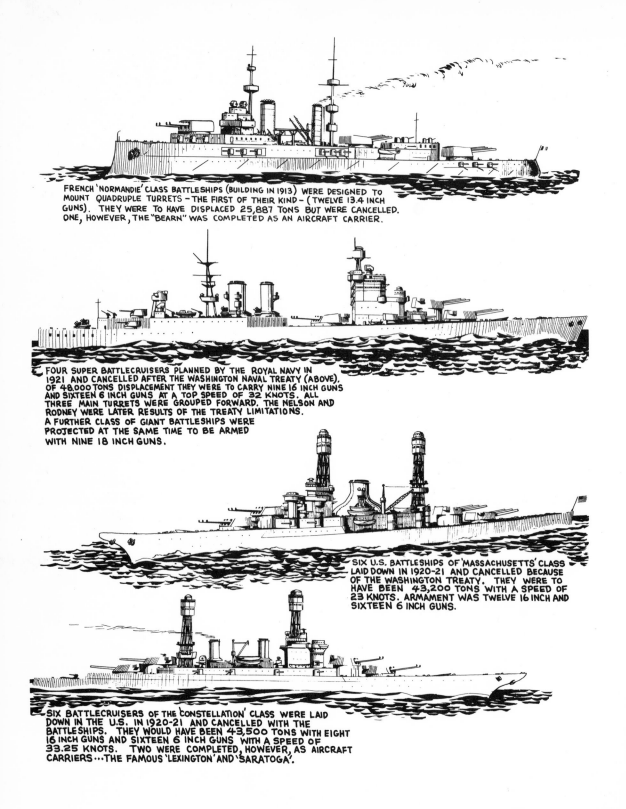

FRENCH 'NORMANDIE' CLASS BATTLESHIPS (BUILDING IN 1913) WERE DESIGNED TO
MOUNT QUADRUPLE TURRETS - THE FIRST OF THEIR KIND - (TWELVE 13.4 INCH
GUNS). THEY WERE TO HAVE DISPLACED 25,887 TONS BUT WERE CANCELLED.
ONE, HOWEVER, THE "BEARN" WAS COMPLETED AS AN AIRCRAFT CARRIER.

FOUR SUPER BATTLECRUISERS PLANNED BY THE ROYAL NAVY IN
1921 AND CANCELLED AFTER THE WASHINGTON NAVAL TREATY (ABOVE),
OF 48,000 TONS DISPLACEMENT THEY WERE TO CARRY NINE 16 INCH GUNS
AND SIXTEEN 6 INCH GUNS AT A TOP SPEED OF 32 KNOTS. ALL
THREE MAIN TURRETS WERE GROUPED FORWARD. THE NELSON AND
RODNEY WERE LATER RESULTS OF THE TREATY LIMITATIONS.
A FURTHER CLASS OF GIANT BATTLESHIPS WERE
PROJECTED AT THE SAME TIME TO BE ARMED
WITH NINE 18 INCH GUNS.

SIX U.S. BATTLESHIPS OF 'MASSACHUSETTS' CLASS
LAID DOWN IN 1920-21 AND CANCELLED BECAUSE
OF THE WASHINGTON TREATY. THEY WERE TO
HAVE BEEN 43,200 TONS WITH A SPEED OF
23 KNOTS. ARMAMENT WAS TWELVE 16 INCH AND
SIXTEEN 6 INCH GUNS.

SIX BATTLECRUISERS OF THE 'CONSTELLATION' CLASS WERE LAID
DOWN IN THE U.S. IN 1920-21 AND CANCELLED WITH THE
BATTLESHIPS. THEY WOULD HAVE BEEN 43,500 TONS WITH EIGHT
16 INCH GUNS AND SIXTEEN 6 INCH GUNS WITH A SPEED OF
33.25 KNOTS. TWO WERE COMPLETED, HOWEVER, AS AIRCRAFT
CARRIERS...THE FAMOUS 'LEXINGTON' AND 'SARATOGA'.

J. M. THORNTON

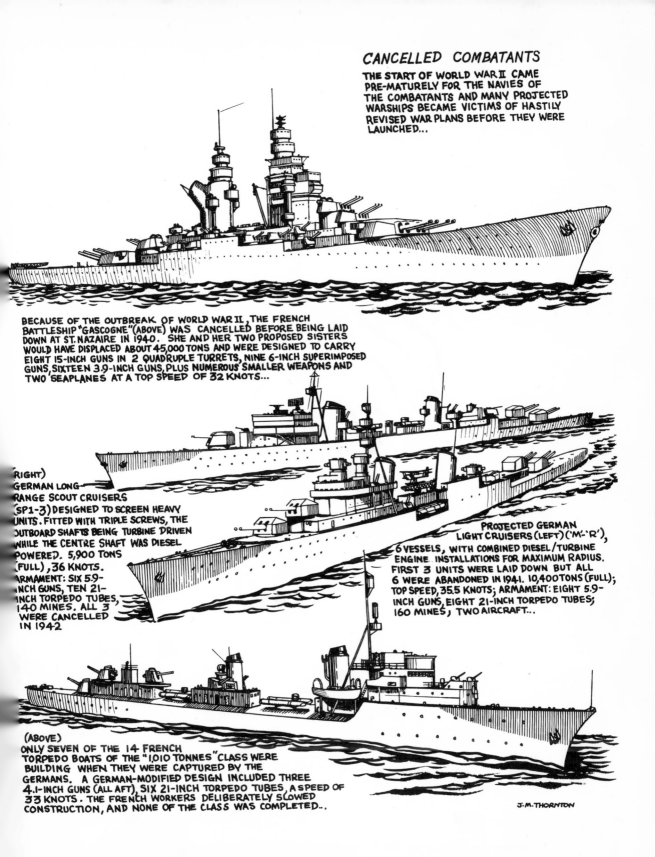

CANCELLED COMBATANTS

THE START OF WORLD WAR II CAME PRE-MATURELY FOR THE NAVIES OF THE COMBATANTS AND MANY PROJECTED WARSHIPS BECAME VICTIMS OF HASTILY REVISED WAR PLANS BEFORE THEY WERE LAUNCHED...

BECAUSE OF THE OUTBREAK OF WORLD WAR II, THE FRENCH BATTLESHIP "GASCOGNE" (ABOVE) WAS CANCELLED BEFORE BEING LAID DOWN AT ST. NAZAIRE IN 1940. SHE AND HER TWO PROPOSED SISTERS WOULD HAVE DISPLACED ABOUT 45,000 TONS AND WERE DESIGNED TO CARRY EIGHT 15-INCH GUNS IN 2 QUADRUPLE TURRETS, NINE 6-INCH SUPERIMPOSED GUNS, SIXTEEN 3.9-INCH GUNS, PLUS NUMEROUS SMALLER WEAPONS AND TWO SEAPLANES AT A TOP SPEED OF 32 KNOTS...

(RIGHT)
GERMAN LONG-RANGE SCOUT CRUISERS (SP1-3) DESIGNED TO SCREEN HEAVY UNITS. FITTED WITH TRIPLE SCREWS, THE OUTBOARD SHAFTS BEING TURBINE DRIVEN WHILE THE CENTRE SHAFT WAS DIESEL POWERED. 5,900 TONS (FULL), 36 KNOTS. ARMAMENT: SIX 5.9-INCH GUNS, TEN 21-INCH TORPEDO TUBES, 140 MINES. ALL 3 WERE CANCELLED IN 1942

PROJECTED GERMAN LIGHT CRUISERS (LEFT) ('M'-'R'), 6 VESSELS, WITH COMBINED DIESEL/TURBINE ENGINE INSTALLATIONS FOR MAXIMUM RADIUS. FIRST 3 UNITS WERE LAID DOWN BUT ALL 6 WERE ABANDONED IN 1941. 10,400 TONS (FULL); TOP SPEED, 35.5 KNOTS; ARMAMENT: EIGHT 5.9-INCH GUNS, EIGHT 21-INCH TORPEDO TUBES; 160 MINES, TWO AIRCRAFT...

(ABOVE)
ONLY SEVEN OF THE 14 FRENCH TORPEDO BOATS OF THE "1,010 TONNES" CLASS WERE BUILDING WHEN THEY WERE CAPTURED BY THE GERMANS. A GERMAN-MODIFIED DESIGN INCLUDED THREE 4.1-INCH GUNS (ALL AFT), SIX 21-INCH TORPEDO TUBES, A SPEED OF 33 KNOTS. THE FRENCH WORKERS DELIBERATELY SLOWED CONSTRUCTION, AND NONE OF THE CLASS WAS COMPLETED...

J.M.THORNTON

GIANTS THAT NEVER SAILED

MANY GREAT SHIPS BUILDING IN THE
YARDS OF THE NATIONS THAT FOUND
THEMSELVES AT WAR IN 1939 WERE
CANCELLED ON THE WAYS BECAUSE
OF SHORTAGE OF MATERIALS AND
ENEMY ACTION, ETC. OTHERS WERE
CANCELLED AS THE WAR REACHED
ITS CONCLUSION AND THEY WERE NO
LONGER NEEDED...

THE CONSTRUCTION OF THREE GIANT BRITISH
AIRCRAFT CARRIERS OF THE "GIBRALTAR"
CLASS... H.M. SHIPS "GIBRALTAR", "MALTA" AND "NEW
ZEALAND", WAS CANCELLED IN 1945 UPON THE
TERMINATION OF HOSTILITIES. OF 45,000 TONS
DISPLACEMENT, THEY WERE DESIGNED TO
CARRY UP TO 100 AIRCRAFT...

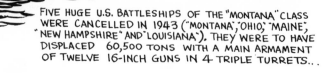

FIVE HUGE U.S. BATTLESHIPS OF THE "MONTANA" CLASS
WERE CANCELLED IN 1943 ("MONTANA", "OHIO", "MAINE",
"NEW HAMPSHIRE" AND "LOUISIANA"). THEY WERE TO HAVE
DISPLACED 60,500 TONS WITH A MAIN ARMAMENT
OF TWELVE 16-INCH GUNS IN 4 TRIPLE TURRETS...

THREE BATTLECRUISERS WERE PROJECTED FOR THE
NETHERLANDS NAVY IN 1939. DESIGNED TO DEFEND
THE DUTCH EAST INDIES THEY WOULD HAVE DIS-
PLACED 28,318 TONS. ARMAMENT WAS TO HAVE
BEEN NINE 11-INCH GUNS (OF GERMAN MANUFACTURE)
WITH A SPEED OF 34 KNOTS. THE OUTBREAK OF
WORLD WAR II ENDED THE PROJECT ....

J.M. THORNTON

CARRIERS "THAT NEVER WERE"

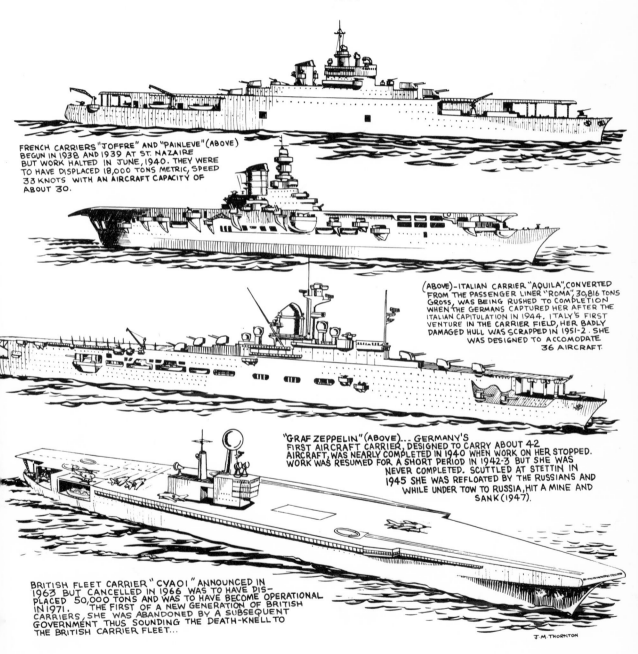

FRENCH CARRIERS "JOFFRE" AND "PAINLEVE" (ABOVE) BEGUN IN 1938 AND 1939 AT ST. NAZAIRE BUT WORK HALTED IN JUNE, 1940. THEY WERE TO HAVE DISPLACED 18,000 TONS METRIC, SPEED 33 KNOTS WITH AN AIRCRAFT CAPACITY OF ABOUT 30.

(ABOVE)-ITALIAN CARRIER "AQUILA", CONVERTED FROM THE PASSENGER LINER "ROMA", 30,816 TONS GROSS, WAS BEING RUSHED TO COMPLETION WHEN THE GERMANS CAPTURED HER AFTER THE ITALIAN CAPITULATION IN 1944. ITALY'S FIRST VENTURE IN THE CARRIER FIELD, HER BADLY DAMAGED HULL WAS SCRAPPED IN 1951-2. SHE WAS DESIGNED TO ACCOMODATE 36 AIRCRAFT.

"GRAF ZEPPELIN" (ABOVE)... GERMANY'S FIRST AIRCRAFT CARRIER, DESIGNED TO CARRY ABOUT 42 AIRCRAFT, WAS NEARLY COMPLETED IN 1940 WHEN WORK ON HER STOPPED. WORK WAS RESUMED FOR A SHORT PERIOD IN 1942-3 BUT SHE WAS NEVER COMPLETED. SCUTTLED AT STETTIN IN 1945 SHE WAS REFLOATED BY THE RUSSIANS AND WHILE UNDER TOW TO RUSSIA, HIT A MINE AND SANK (1947).

BRITISH FLEET CARRIER "CVA01" ANNOUNCED IN 1963 BUT CANCELLED IN 1966 WAS TO HAVE DIS-PLACED 50,000 TONS AND WAS TO HAVE BECOME OPERATIONAL IN 1971. THE FIRST OF A NEW GENERATION OF BRITISH CARRIERS, SHE WAS ABANDONED BY A SUBSEQUENT GOVERNMENT THUS SOUNDING THE DEATH-KNELL TO THE BRITISH CARRIER FLEET...

J.M. THORNTON

PART EIGHT

Deception at Sea

The art of deception at sea has been practiced with resource and ingenuity by both naval designers, 'boffins' and sailors. From the simple 'ruse de guerre' of sailing under false colours to the elaborate construction of an entire false battle squadron, the deception of the enemy has been a foremost tactical objective.

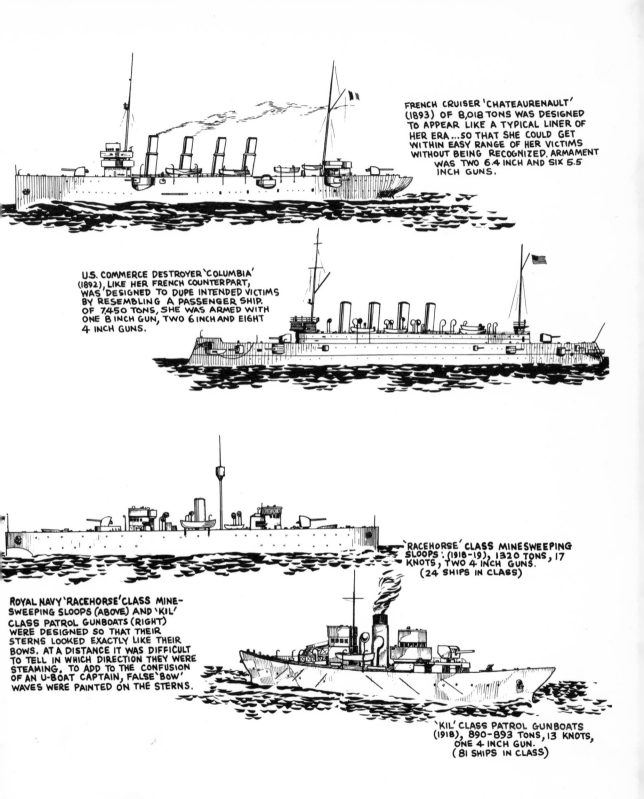

FRENCH CRUISER 'CHATEAURENAULT' (1893) OF 8,018 TONS WAS DESIGNED TO APPEAR LIKE A TYPICAL LINER OF HER ERA...SO THAT SHE COULD GET WITHIN EASY RANGE OF HER VICTIMS WITHOUT BEING RECOGNIZED. ARMAMENT WAS TWO 6.4 INCH AND SIX 5.5 INCH GUNS.

U.S. COMMERCE DESTROYER 'COLUMBIA' (1892), LIKE HER FRENCH COUNTERPART, WAS DESIGNED TO DUPE INTENDED VICTIMS BY RESEMBLING A PASSENGER SHIP. OF 7450 TONS, SHE WAS ARMED WITH ONE 8 INCH GUN, TWO 6 INCH AND EIGHT 4 INCH GUNS.

'RACEHORSE' CLASS MINESWEEPING SLOOPS: (1918-19), 1320 TONS, 17 KNOTS, TWO 4 INCH GUNS. (24 SHIPS IN CLASS)

ROYAL NAVY 'RACEHORSE' CLASS MINE-SWEEPING SLOOPS (ABOVE) AND 'KIL' CLASS PATROL GUNBOATS (RIGHT) WERE DESIGNED SO THAT THEIR STERNS LOOKED EXACTLY LIKE THEIR BOWS. AT A DISTANCE IT WAS DIFFICULT TO TELL IN WHICH DIRECTION THEY WERE STEAMING. TO ADD TO THE CONFUSION OF AN U-BOAT CAPTAIN, FALSE 'BOW' WAVES WERE PAINTED ON THE STERNS.

'KIL' CLASS PATROL GUNBOATS (1918), 890-893 TONS, 13 KNOTS, ONE 4 INCH GUN. (81 SHIPS IN CLASS)

THE GERMAN AUXILIARY CRUISER "PRINZ EITEL FRIEDRICH" (EX-NORD DEUTSCHER LLOYD LINER) ESCAPED ALLIED CAPTURE FOR 7 MONTHS BEFORE VOLUNTARY INTERNMENT AT NEWPORT NEWS ON 9 APRIL, 1915. SHE RECEIVED HER GUNS FROM A GERMAN CRUISER IN THE PACIFIC, SAILED WITH VON SPEE, ESCAPED FROM THE BATTLE OFF 'THE FALKLAND ISLANDS' AND SANK OR CAPTURED 10 ALLIED SHIPS. TO ELUDE CAPTURE ONE SIDE WAS PAINTED WHITE, THE OTHER BLACK. SHE EVENTUALLY FELL IN WITH A BRITISH CRUISER WHICH GAVE CHASE. STEAMING INTO A FOG PATCH SHE TURNED ABOUT. WHEN THE CRUISER SIGHTED A WHITE SHIP COMING TOWARDS HER, SHE SIGNALLED "HAVE YOU SEEN A BLACK SHIP?" TO WHICH THE RAIDER REPLIED IN THE AFFIRMATIVE "18 MILES TO THE WEST".... AND MADE GOOD HER ESCAPE WHILE THE CRUISER STEAMED WEST IN VAIN PURSUIT!

IN 1917 SEVERAL BRITISH SUBMARINES WERE FITTED WITH OCCULTING LIGHTS AND SECURED AT NIGHT TO THE GOODWINS-SNOU NET BARRAGE. THUS DISGUISED AS BUOYS, THEY HOPED TO LURE SURFACED U-BOATS WITHIN RANGE OF THEIR TORPEDOES...

THE "WATER DONKEY"- GERMAN U-BOAT DEVICE TO DECEIVE ALLIED ESCORTS IN WORLD WAR II. IT WAS DESIGNED AS A MINIATURE U-BOAT WITH AN EXACT REPLICA OF A CONNING TOWER AND WAS TOWED JUST BELOW THE SURFACE BY AN ELECTRIC CABLE FROM THE PARENT U-BOAT. WHEN DETECTED BY ALLIED ESCORTS OR AIRCRAFT, THE U-BOAT C.O. STARTED MACHINERY IN THE DUMMY TO MAKE A CAVITATION NOISE. IF ATTACKED IT COULD RELEASE AIR BUBBLES, OIL AND DEBRIS AND COULD BE FLOODED AND SUNK WHILE THE REAL U-BOAT ESCAPED. ANOTHER DECOY WAS THE PERISCOPE MINE (A) WHICH COULD BE RELEASED BY THE U-BOAT.

1945 - GERMAN 500-TON U-BOAT COMPLETELY COVERED WITH RUBBER! THE RUBBER COATING WHICH WAS 'PITTED' WITH CIRCULAR DEPRESSIONS, WAS DESIGNED TO BAFFLE ALLIED ASDIC. POST-WAR TESTS PROVED THAT IT WAS INEFFECTIVE...

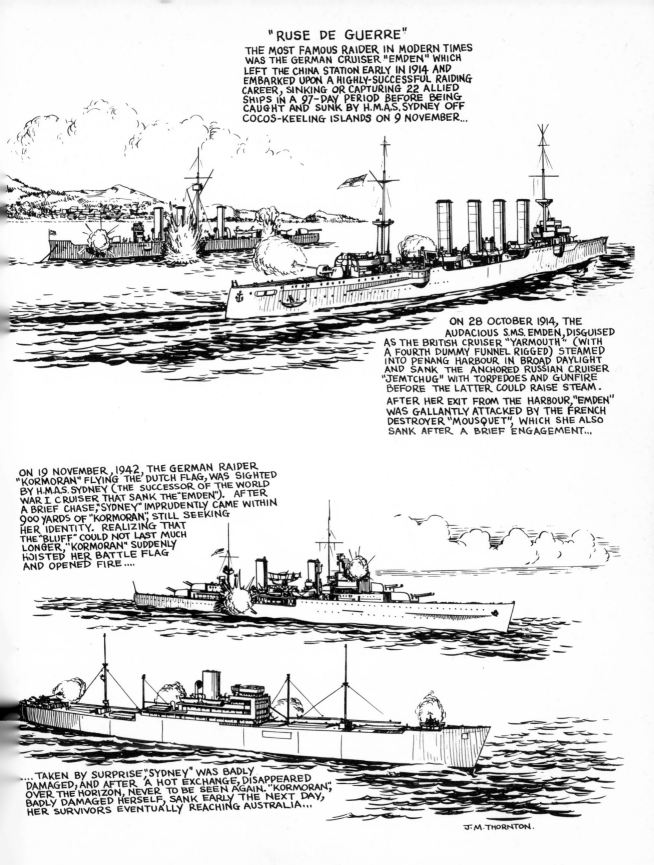

"RUSE DE GUERRE"

THE MOST FAMOUS RAIDER IN MODERN TIMES WAS THE GERMAN CRUISER "EMDEN" WHICH LEFT THE CHINA STATION EARLY IN 1914 AND EMBARKED UPON A HIGHLY-SUCCESSFUL RAIDING CAREER, SINKING OR CAPTURING 22 ALLIED SHIPS IN A 97-DAY PERIOD BEFORE BEING CAUGHT AND SUNK BY H.M.A.S. SYDNEY OFF COCOS-KEELING ISLANDS ON 9 NOVEMBER...

ON 28 OCTOBER 1914, THE AUDACIOUS S.M.S. EMDEN, DISGUISED AS THE BRITISH CRUISER "YARMOUTH" (WITH A FOURTH DUMMY FUNNEL RIGGED) STEAMED INTO PENANG HARBOUR IN BROAD DAYLIGHT AND SANK THE ANCHORED RUSSIAN CRUISER "JEMTCHUG" WITH TORPEDOES AND GUNFIRE BEFORE THE LATTER COULD RAISE STEAM.

AFTER HER EXIT FROM THE HARBOUR, "EMDEN" WAS GALLANTLY ATTACKED BY THE FRENCH DESTROYER "MOUSQUET", WHICH SHE ALSO SANK AFTER A BRIEF ENGAGEMENT...

ON 19 NOVEMBER, 1942, THE GERMAN RAIDER "KORMORAN" FLYING THE DUTCH FLAG, WAS SIGHTED BY H.M.A.S. SYDNEY (THE SUCCESSOR OF THE WORLD WAR I CRUISER THAT SANK THE "EMDEN"). AFTER A BRIEF CHASE, "SYDNEY" IMPRUDENTLY CAME WITHIN 900 YARDS OF "KORMORAN", STILL SEEKING HER IDENTITY. REALIZING THAT THE "BLUFF" COULD NOT LAST MUCH LONGER, "KORMORAN" SUDDENLY HOISTED HER BATTLE FLAG AND OPENED FIRE....

....TAKEN BY SURPRISE "SYDNEY" WAS BADLY DAMAGED, AND AFTER A HOT EXCHANGE, DISAPPEARED OVER THE HORIZON, NEVER TO BE SEEN AGAIN. "KORMORAN", BADLY DAMAGED HERSELF, SANK EARLY THE NEXT DAY, HER SURVIVORS EVENTUALLY REACHING AUSTRALIA...

J.M. THORNTON.

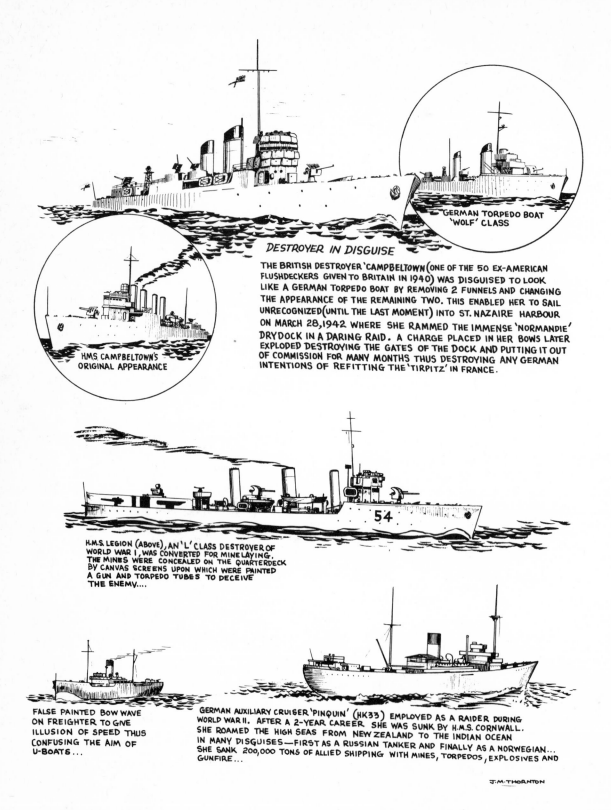

GERMAN TORPEDO BOAT
'WOLF' CLASS

HMS CAMPBELTOWN'S
ORIGINAL APPEARANCE

DESTROYER IN DISGUISE

THE BRITISH DESTROYER 'CAMPBELTOWN (ONE OF THE 50 EX-AMERICAN
FLUSHDECKERS GIVEN TO BRITAIN IN 1940) WAS DISGUISED TO LOOK
LIKE A GERMAN TORPEDO BOAT BY REMOVING 2 FUNNELS AND CHANGING
THE APPEARANCE OF THE REMAINING TWO. THIS ENABLED HER TO SAIL
UNRECOGNIZED (UNTIL THE LAST MOMENT) INTO ST. NAZAIRE HARBOUR
ON MARCH 28,1942 WHERE SHE RAMMED THE IMMENSE 'NORMANDIE'
DRYDOCK IN A DARING RAID. A CHARGE PLACED IN HER BOWS LATER
EXPLODED DESTROYING THE GATES OF THE DOCK AND PUTTING IT OUT
OF COMMISSION FOR MANY MONTHS THUS DESTROYING ANY GERMAN
INTENTIONS OF REFITTING THE 'TIRPITZ' IN FRANCE.

H.M.S. LEGION (ABOVE), AN 'L' CLASS DESTROYER OF
WORLD WAR I, WAS CONVERTED FOR MINELAYING.
THE MINES WERE CONCEALED ON THE QUARTERDECK
BY CANVAS SCREENS UPON WHICH WERE PAINTED
A GUN AND TORPEDO TUBES TO DECEIVE
THE ENEMY....

FALSE PAINTED BOW WAVE
ON FREIGHTER TO GIVE
ILLUSION OF SPEED THUS
CONFUSING THE AIM OF
U-BOATS...

GERMAN AUXILIARY CRUISER 'PINQUIN' (HK33) EMPLOYED AS A RAIDER DURING
WORLD WAR II. AFTER A 2-YEAR CAREER SHE WAS SUNK BY H.M.S. CORNWALL.
SHE ROAMED THE HIGH SEAS FROM NEW ZEALAND TO THE INDIAN OCEAN
IN MANY DISGUISES—FIRST AS A RUSSIAN TANKER AND FINALLY AS A NORWEGIAN...
SHE SANK 200,000 TONS OF ALLIED SHIPPING WITH MINES, TORPEDOS, EXPLOSIVES AND
GUNFIRE...

J.M.THORNTON

IN WORLD WAR I, BRITISH NAVAL SUPERIORITY BECAME SO SLIM THAT THE ADMIRALTY HAD DIFFICULTY IN MAINTAINING A SUPERIOR BATTLE FLEET IN READINESS AT ALL TIMES. TO DUPE THE ENEMY INTO THINKING THAT THE GRAND FLEET WAS ALWAYS AT FULL STRENGTH, A FLEET OF TEN DUMMY BATTLESHIPS WAS CREATED...IN REALITY, OLD MERCHANT SHIPS, SECRETLY DISGUISED WITH CANVAS AND WOOD. ORIGINALLY NAMED THE "10TH BATTLE SQUADRON" AND MANNED BY R.N.R. PERSONNEL, THESE MOCK-UP BATTLESHIPS LATER BECAME KNOWN AS THE "SPECIAL SERVICE SQUADRON".

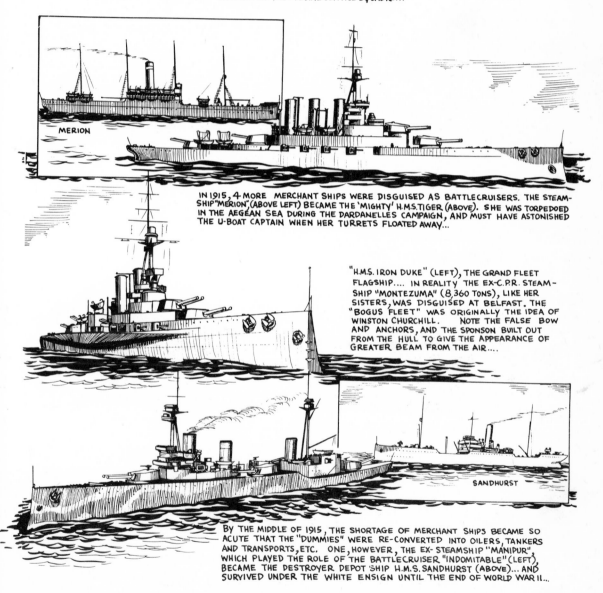

MERION

IN 1915, 4 MORE MERCHANT SHIPS WERE DISGUISED AS BATTLECRUISERS. THE STEAMSHIP "MERION" (ABOVE LEFT) BECAME THE 'MIGHTY' H.M.S. TIGER (ABOVE). SHE WAS TORPEDOED IN THE AEGÉAN SEA DURING THE DARDANELLES CAMPAIGN, AND MUST HAVE ASTONISHED THE U-BOAT CAPTAIN WHEN HER TURRETS FLOATED AWAY...

"H.M.S. IRON DUKE" (LEFT), THE GRAND FLEET FLAGSHIP.... IN REALITY THE EX-C.P.R. STEAMSHIP "MONTEZUMA" (8,360 TONS), LIKE HER SISTERS, WAS DISGUISED AT BELFAST. THE "BOGUS FLEET" WAS ORIGINALLY THE IDEA OF WINSTON CHURCHILL. NOTE THE FALSE BOW AND ANCHORS, AND THE SPONSON BUILT OUT FROM THE HULL TO GIVE THE APPEARANCE OF GREATER BEAM FROM THE AIR....

SANDHURST

BY THE MIDDLE OF 1915, THE SHORTAGE OF MERCHANT SHIPS BECAME SO ACUTE THAT THE "DUMMIES" WERE RE-CONVERTED INTO OILERS, TANKERS AND TRANSPORTS, ETC. ONE, HOWEVER, THE EX-STEAMSHIP "MANIPUR", WHICH PLAYED THE ROLE OF THE BATTLECRUISER "INDOMITABLE" (LEFT), BECAME THE DESTROYER DEPOT SHIP H.M.S. SANDHURST (ABOVE)... AND SURVIVED UNDER THE WHITE ENSIGN UNTIL THE END OF WORLD WAR II...

ON 27 OCT. 1914, H.M.S. AUDACIOUS (BATTLESHIP) STRUCK A MINE (LAID BY
THE GERMAN AUXILIARY MINELAYER "BERLIN") WHILE TAKING PART IN FIRING
PRACTICE IN THE ATLANTIC. SEVERAL ATTEMPTS WERE MADE TO SAVE HER
BUT SHE EVENTUALLY SANK, THUS REDUCING THE NUMERICAL STRENGTH OF THE
BRITISH FLEET IN RELATION TO THAT OF GERMANY. IN ORDER TO CONCEAL THIS WEAKNESS,
HER LOSS WAS DENIED AND THE C.P.R. MERCHANT SHIP "MONTCALM" (5,500 TONS) WAS
DISGUISED TO REPRESENT THE BATTLESHIP. HER LOSS WAS NOT ADMITTED UNTIL
AFTER THE WAR....

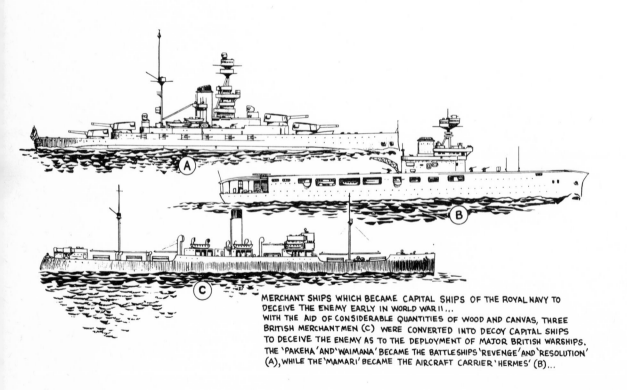

MERCHANT SHIPS WHICH BECAME CAPITAL SHIPS OF THE ROYAL NAVY TO
DECEIVE THE ENEMY EARLY IN WORLD WAR II...
WITH THE AID OF CONSIDERABLE QUANTITIES OF WOOD AND CANVAS, THREE
BRITISH MERCHANTMEN (C) WERE CONVERTED INTO DECOY CAPITAL SHIPS
TO DECEIVE THE ENEMY AS TO THE DEPLOYMENT OF MAJOR BRITISH WARSHIPS.
THE 'PAKEHA' AND 'WAIMANA' BECAME THE BATTLESHIPS 'REVENGE' AND 'RESOLUTION'
(A), WHILE THE 'MAMARI' BECAME THE AIRCRAFT CARRIER 'HERMES' (B)...

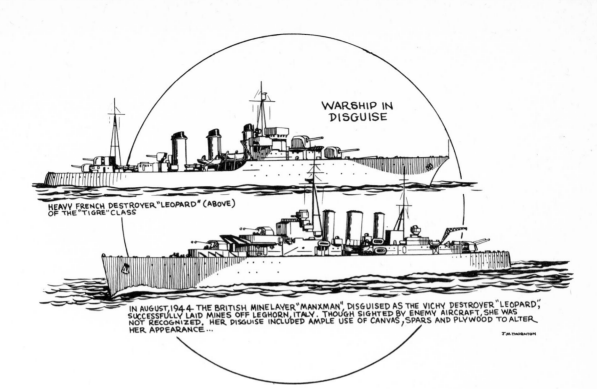

WARSHIP IN
DISGUISE

HEAVY FRENCH DESTROYER "LEOPARD" (ABOVE)
OF THE "TIGRE" CLASS

IN AUGUST, 1944 THE BRITISH MINELAYER "MANXMAN", DISGUISED AS THE VICHY DESTROYER "LEOPARD",
SUCCESSFULLY LAID MINES OFF LEGHORN, ITALY. THOUGH SIGHTED BY ENEMY AIRCRAFT, SHE WAS
NOT RECOGNIZED. HER DISGUISE INCLUDED AMPLE USE OF CANVAS, SPARS AND PLYWOOD TO ALTER
HER APPEARANCE...

J.M.THORNTON

PART NINE

Merchantmen at Arms

Up to the early nineteenth century it was commonplace for merchant ships to double as men-of-war, but as ships became more complex and specialized, the employment of merchant ships as naval auxiliaries became increasingly difficult. This did not mean the end of merchantmen doing sterling work as converted naval units. Some have been ear-marked as potential auxiliaries during their building stage and specially strengthened, while others require extensive refitting, and in two World Wars many merchant ships have been taken into naval service. Some have distinguished themselves in battle.

LINERS AT WAR

MANY FAST LINERS "JOINED THE NAVY" EARLY IN BOTH
WORLD WARS TO SERVE AS ARMED MERCHANT CRUISERS
(AMC's). THEY WERE ARMED AND USED TO PATROL THE
SEA LANES AND TO PROTECT CONVOYS FROM RAIDERS.
WHEN THIS THREAT WAS ELIMINATED THEY WERE
CONVERTED TO OTHER EMPLOYMENT...

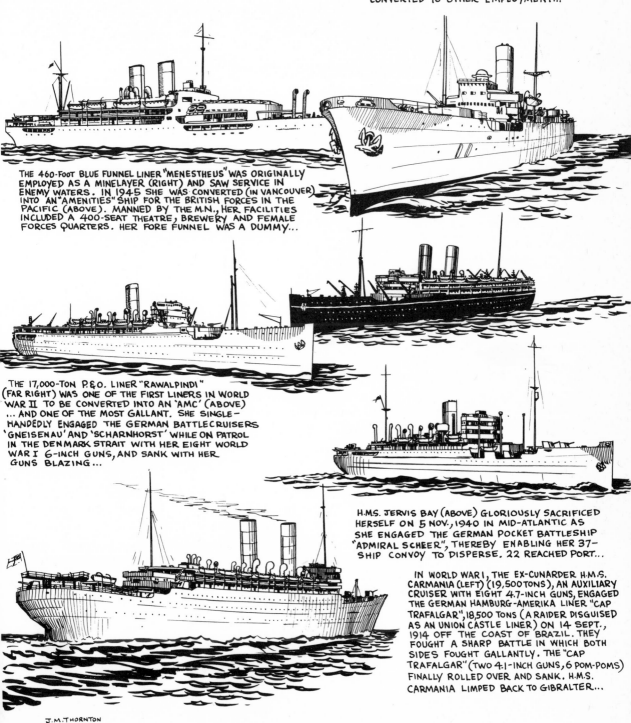

THE 460-FOOT BLUE FUNNEL LINER "MENESTHEUS" WAS ORIGINALLY
EMPLOYED AS A MINELAYER (RIGHT) AND SAW SERVICE IN
ENEMY WATERS. IN 1945 SHE WAS CONVERTED (IN VANCOUVER)
INTO AN "AMENITIES" SHIP FOR THE BRITISH FORCES IN THE
PACIFIC (ABOVE). MANNED BY THE M.N., HER FACILITIES
INCLUDED A 400-SEAT THEATRE, BREWERY AND FEMALE
FORCES QUARTERS. HER FORE FUNNEL WAS A DUMMY...

THE 17,000-TON P.&O. LINER "RAWALPINDI"
(FAR RIGHT) WAS ONE OF THE FIRST LINERS IN WORLD
WAR II TO BE CONVERTED INTO AN 'AMC' (ABOVE)
... AND ONE OF THE MOST GALLANT. SHE SINGLE-
HANDEDLY ENGAGED THE GERMAN BATTLECRUISERS
'GNEISENAU' AND 'SCHARNHORST' WHILE ON PATROL
IN THE DENMARK STRAIT WITH HER EIGHT WORLD
WAR I 6-INCH GUNS, AND SANK WITH HER
GUNS BLAZING...

H.M.S. JERVIS BAY (ABOVE) GLORIOUSLY SACRIFICED
HERSELF ON 5 NOV., 1940 IN MID-ATLANTIC AS
SHE ENGAGED THE GERMAN POCKET BATTLESHIP
"ADMIRAL SCHEER", THEREBY ENABLING HER 37-
SHIP CONVOY TO DISPERSE. 22 REACHED PORT...

IN WORLD WAR I, THE EX-CUNARDER H.M.S.
CARMANIA (LEFT) (19,500 TONS), AN AUXILIARY
CRUISER WITH EIGHT 4.7-INCH GUNS, ENGAGED
THE GERMAN HAMBURG-AMERIKA LINER "CAP
TRAFALGAR", 18,500 TONS (A RAIDER DISGUISED
AS AN UNION CASTLE LINER) ON 14 SEPT.,
1914 OFF THE COAST OF BRAZIL. THEY
FOUGHT A SHARP BATTLE IN WHICH BOTH
SIDES FOUGHT GALLANTLY. THE "CAP
TRAFALGAR" (TWO 4.1-INCH GUNS, 6 POM-POMS)
FINALLY ROLLED OVER AND SANK. H.M.S.
CARMANIA LIMPED BACK TO GIBRALTER...

J.M. THORNTON

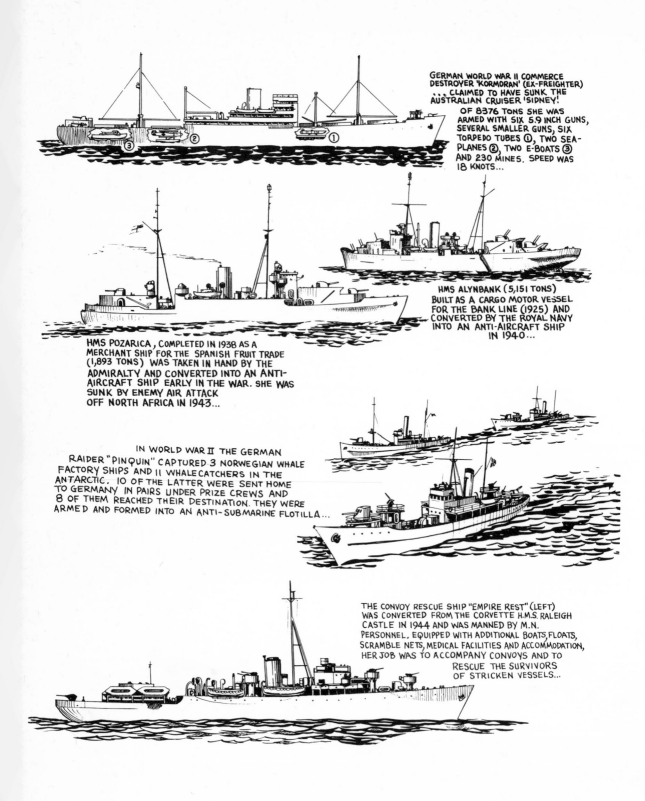

GERMAN WORLD WAR II COMMERCE
DESTROYER 'KORMORAN' (EX-FREIGHTER)
... CLAIMED TO HAVE SUNK THE
AUSTRALIAN CRUISER 'SIDNEY!'
OF 8376 TONS SHE WAS
ARMED WITH SIX 5.9 INCH GUNS,
SEVERAL SMALLER GUNS, SIX
TORPEDO TUBES ①, TWO SEA-
PLANES ②, TWO E-BOATS ③
AND 230 MINES. SPEED WAS
18 KNOTS...

HMS ALYNBANK (5,151 TONS)
BUILT AS A CARGO MOTOR VESSEL
FOR THE BANK LINE (1925) AND
CONVERTED BY THE ROYAL NAVY
INTO AN ANTI-AIRCRAFT SHIP
IN 1940...

HMS POZARICA, COMPLETED IN 1938 AS A
MERCHANT SHIP FOR THE SPANISH FRUIT TRADE
(1,893 TONS) WAS TAKEN IN HAND BY THE
ADMIRALTY AND CONVERTED INTO AN ANTI-
AIRCRAFT SHIP EARLY IN THE WAR. SHE WAS
SUNK BY ENEMY AIR ATTACK
OFF NORTH AFRICA IN 1943...

IN WORLD WAR II THE GERMAN
RAIDER "PINQUIN" CAPTURED 3 NORWEGIAN WHALE
FACTORY SHIPS AND 11 WHALECATCHERS IN THE
ANTARCTIC. 10 OF THE LATTER WERE SENT HOME
TO GERMANY IN PAIRS UNDER PRIZE CREWS AND
8 OF THEM REACHED THEIR DESTINATION. THEY WERE
ARMED AND FORMED INTO AN ANTI-SUBMARINE FLOTILLA...

THE CONVOY RESCUE SHIP "EMPIRE REST" (LEFT)
WAS CONVERTED FROM THE CORVETTE H.M.S. RALEIGH
CASTLE IN 1944 AND WAS MANNED BY M.N.
PERSONNEL. EQUIPPED WITH ADDITIONAL BOATS, FLOATS,
SCRAMBLE NETS, MEDICAL FACILITIES AND ACCOMMODATION,
HER JOB WAS TO ACCOMPANY CONVOYS AND TO
RESCUE THE SURVIVORS
OF STRICKEN VESSELS...

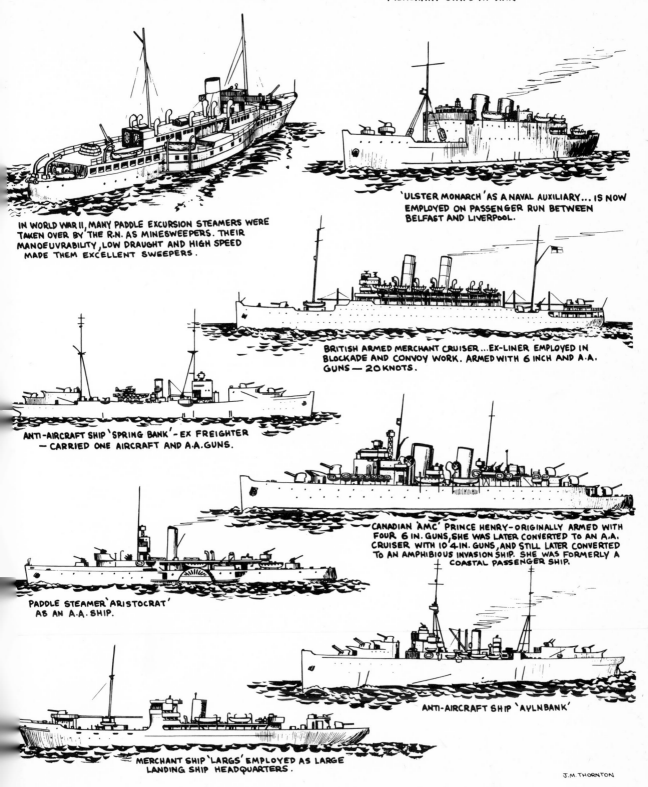

IN WORLD WAR II, MANY PADDLE EXCURSION STEAMERS WERE
TAKEN OVER BY THE R.N. AS MINESWEEPERS. THEIR
MANOEUVRABILITY, LOW DRAUGHT AND HIGH SPEED
MADE THEM EXCELLENT SWEEPERS.

'ULSTER MONARCH' AS A NAVAL AUXILIARY... IS NOW
EMPLOYED ON PASSENGER RUN BETWEEN
BELFAST AND LIVERPOOL.

BRITISH ARMED MERCHANT CRUISER... EX-LINER EMPLOYED IN
BLOCKADE AND CONVOY WORK. ARMED WITH 6 INCH AND A.A.
GUNS — 20 KNOTS.

ANTI-AIRCRAFT SHIP 'SPRING BANK' - EX FREIGHTER
— CARRIED ONE AIRCRAFT AND A.A. GUNS.

CANADIAN 'AMC' PRINCE HENRY - ORIGINALLY ARMED WITH
FOUR 6 IN. GUNS, SHE WAS LATER CONVERTED TO AN A.A.
CRUISER WITH 10 4-IN. GUNS, AND STILL LATER CONVERTED
TO AN AMPHIBIOUS INVASION SHIP. SHE WAS FORMERLY A
COASTAL PASSENGER SHIP.

PADDLE STEAMER 'ARISTOCRAT'
AS AN A.A. SHIP.

ANTI-AIRCRAFT SHIP 'AYLNBANK'

MERCHANT SHIP 'LARGS' EMPLOYED AS LARGE
LANDING SHIP HEADQUARTERS.

J.M. THORNTON

MAKESHIFT CARRIERS

DURING THE EARLY PART OF WORLD WAR II THE LACK OF ESCORTS AND AIR COVER IN THE NORTH ATLANTIC BECAME CRITICAL. THE ROYAL NAVY, DESPERATELY SHORT OF AIRCRAFT CARRIERS, QUICKLY FITTED A NUMBER OF MERCHANT SHIPS WITH FLIGHT DECKS TO "CLOSE THE GAP" UNTIL THE FAMOUS "WOOLWORTH" CARRIERS BECAME AVAILABLE FROM AMERICA...

THE UNION-CASTLE LINER "PRETORIA CASTLE" WAS CONVERTED INTO AN ARMED MERCHANT CRUISER IN 1940 (ABOVE) AND LATER (1943) INTO AN ESCORT CARRIER (LEFT). SHE WAS EMPLOYED MAINLY ON TRAINING AND EXPERIMENTAL DUTIES. SHE SURVIVED THE WAR AND WAS RECONSTRUCTED TO HER ORIGINAL ROLE AND RENAMED "WARWICK CASTLE" IN 1946...

THE FIRST OF HER KIND ... H.M.S. AUDACITY (5,537 TONS), FORMERLY THE GERMAN SHIP "M.V. HANNOVER", SHE WAS CAPTURED BY H.M.S. DUNEDIN AND H.M.C.S. ASSINIBOINE OFF SAN DOMINGO IN FEB., 1940. FITTED WITH A 420-FOOT FLIGHT DECK, SHE CARRIED SIX "MARTLET" FIGHTERS. AS THERE WAS NO HANGAR, HER AIRCRAFT WERE STOWED ON DECK. SHE WAS SUNK BY A U-BOAT ON 21 DEC., 1941 ABOUT 500 MILES WEST OF CAPE FINISTERRE...

"RAPANA"

IN EARLY 1941 THE ADMIRALTY INTRODUCED THE "C.A.M." SHIPS.... (CATAPULT ARMED MERCHANTMEN). SELECTED MERCHANT SHIPS WERE FITTED WITH A CATAPULT AND AN HURRICANE FIGHTER TO DEAL WITH ENEMY BOMBERS. ON COMPLETION OF THEIR MISSIONS, THE AIRCRAFT EITHER LANDED ASHORE OR "DITCHED" AT SEA.

LATER IN THE WAR THE "M.A.C." SHIPS (MERCHANT AIRCRAFT CARRIERS) WERE INTRODUCED, (LEFT). THEY WERE GRAIN SHIPS FITTED WITH FLIGHT DECKS AND AIRCRAFT, AND WORE THE RED ENSIGN. THEY PROVIDED AIR PROTECTION FOR THEIR CONVOYS...

J. M. THORNTON

PART TEN

Yachts at War

No more peaceful type of vessel can be imagined than the private steam yacht with its graceful lines, white hull and burnished teak upper works. Yet in time of war many of this type of pleasure craft have served their colours as auxiliary men-of-war, some as first line fighting ships, and even as flag ships!

H.M.C.S. STADACONA

H.M.C.S. STADACONA
'THE MOST NOTORIOUS SHIP TO SERVE IN THE R.C.N.'

BUILT AS A 798 TON YACHT IN PHILA-
DELPHIA IN 1893 SHE WAS REPORTED
TO HAVE FIRED THE FIRST SHOT AT THE
BATTLE OF MANILA BAY IN THE SPANISH-
AMERICAN WAR AS THE U.S. SHIP 'WASP'.
SHE LATER CAME UNDER BRITISH REGISTRY
EARLY IN THE GREAT WAR WHEN A
WEALTHY CANADIAN PRESENTED HER TO
THE CANADIAN GOVERNMENT. SHE WAS
NAMED 'H.M.C.S. STADACONA' AND SERVED AS
A PATROL AND ESCORT VESSEL OUT OF
HALIFAX. AFTER THE WAR SHE WAS SOLD
AND RAN ILLEGAL LIQUOR DURING THE
PROHIBITION ERA UNDER THE NAME 'KUYAKUZNT'.
LATER SHE TURNED RESPECTABLE AND BECAME
A YACHT AGAIN AND RENAMED 'LADY STIMSON'.
LATER SHE WAS RENAMED 'MOONLIGHT
MAID' BY A NEW OWNER. SHE WAS
SOLD TO THE U.S. GOVERNMENT AS A
TOWING AND TRANSPORT VESSEL SAILING
TO ALASKA AND THE ALEUTIANS AND
FINALLY PUT TO THE TORCH AND SCRAPPED
IN SEATTLE EARLY IN 1948.

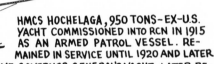

HMCS HOCHELAGA, 950 TONS—EX-U.S.
YACHT COMMISSIONED INTO RCN IN 1915
AS AN ARMED PATROL VESSEL. RE-
MAINED IN SERVICE UNTIL 1920 AND LATER
BECAME GOVERNOR-GENERAL'S YACHT. LATER BE-
CAME A FERRY RUNNING BETWEEN PICTOU AND
PRINCE EDWARD ISLAND UNTIL 1942.

J.M. THORNTON

ONE OF THE ODDEST YACHT-CON-
VERSIONS DURING THE WAR WAS THE
HARBOUR DEFENCE VESSEL H.M.S. DUENA
(LEFT), ARMED WITH A 3-PDR. AND 3 MACHINE
GUNS, HER HULL-LINES REVEALED HER
AS A DISMASTED FORMER SAILING YACHT...

J. M. THORNTON

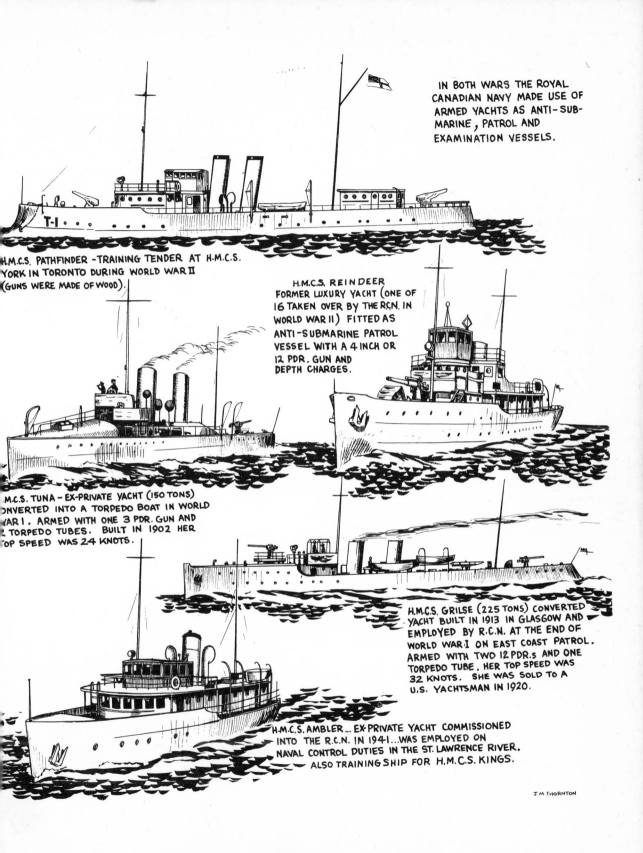

IN BOTH WARS THE ROYAL CANADIAN NAVY MADE USE OF ARMED YACHTS AS ANTI-SUBMARINE, PATROL AND EXAMINATION VESSELS.

H.M.C.S. PATHFINDER -TRAINING TENDER AT H.M.C.S. YORK IN TORONTO DURING WORLD WAR II (GUNS WERE MADE OF WOOD).

H.M.C.S. REINDEER FORMER LUXURY YACHT (ONE OF 16 TAKEN OVER BY THE R.C.N. IN WORLD WAR II) FITTED AS ANTI-SUBMARINE PATROL VESSEL WITH A 4 INCH OR 12 PDR. GUN AND DEPTH CHARGES.

H.M.C.S. TUNA - EX-PRIVATE YACHT (150 TONS) CONVERTED INTO A TORPEDO BOAT IN WORLD WAR I. ARMED WITH ONE 3 PDR. GUN AND 2 TORPEDO TUBES. BUILT IN 1902 HER TOP SPEED WAS 24 KNOTS.

H.M.C.S. GRILSE (225 TONS) CONVERTED YACHT BUILT IN 1913 IN GLASGOW AND EMPLOYED BY R.C.N. AT THE END OF WORLD WAR I ON EAST COAST PATROL. ARMED WITH TWO 12 PDR.s AND ONE TORPEDO TUBE. HER TOP SPEED WAS 32 KNOTS. SHE WAS SOLD TO A U.S. YACHTSMAN IN 1920.

H.M.C.S. AMBLER ... EX-PRIVATE YACHT COMMISSIONED INTO THE R.C.N. IN 1941...WAS EMPLOYED ON NAVAL CONTROL DUTIES IN THE ST. LAWRENCE RIVER, ALSO TRAINING SHIP FOR H.M.C.S. KINGS.

J.M.THORNTON

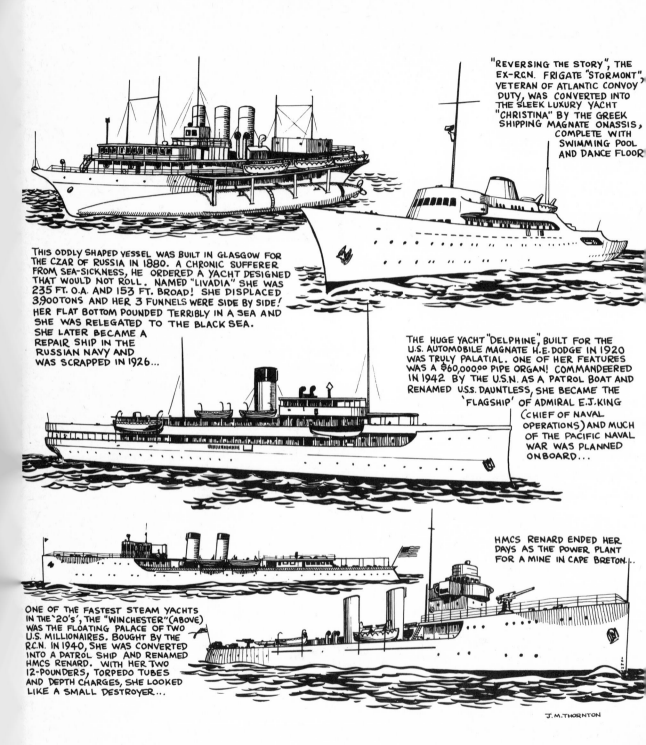

"REVERSING THE STORY", THE EX-R.C.N. FRIGATE "STORMONT", VETERAN OF ATLANTIC CONVOY DUTY, WAS CONVERTED INTO THE SLEEK LUXURY YACHT "CHRISTINA" BY THE GREEK SHIPPING MAGNATE ONASSIS, COMPLETE WITH SWIMMING POOL AND DANCE FLOOR

THIS ODDLY SHAPED VESSEL WAS BUILT IN GLASGOW FOR THE CZAR OF RUSSIA IN 1880. A CHRONIC SUFFERER FROM SEA-SICKNESS, HE ORDERED A YACHT DESIGNED THAT WOULD NOT ROLL. NAMED "LIVADIA" SHE WAS 235 FT. O.A. AND 153 FT. BROAD! SHE DISPLACED 3,900 TONS AND HER 3 FUNNELS WERE SIDE BY SIDE! HER FLAT BOTTOM POUNDED TERRIBLY IN A SEA AND SHE WAS RELEGATED TO THE BLACK SEA. SHE LATER BECAME A REPAIR SHIP IN THE RUSSIAN NAVY AND WAS SCRAPPED IN 1926...

THE HUGE YACHT "DELPHINE", BUILT FOR THE U.S. AUTOMOBILE MAGNATE H.E.DODGE IN 1920 WAS TRULY PALATIAL. ONE OF HER FEATURES WAS A $60,000.00 PIPE ORGAN! COMMANDEERED IN 1942 BY THE U.S.N. AS A PATROL BOAT AND RENAMED U.S.S. DAUNTLESS, SHE BECAME THE 'FLAGSHIP' OF ADMIRAL E.J.KING (CHIEF OF NAVAL OPERATIONS) AND MUCH OF THE PACIFIC NAVAL WAR WAS PLANNED ONBOARD...

HMCS RENARD ENDED HER DAYS AS THE POWER PLANT FOR A MINE IN CAPE BRETON...

ONE OF THE FASTEST STEAM YACHTS IN THE '20's', THE "WINCHESTER" (ABOVE) WAS THE FLOATING PALACE OF TWO U.S. MILLIONAIRES. BOUGHT BY THE R.C.N. IN 1940, SHE WAS CONVERTED INTO A PATROL SHIP AND RENAMED HMCS RENARD. WITH HER TWO 12-POUNDERS, TORPEDO TUBES AND DEPTH CHARGES, SHE LOOKED LIKE A SMALL DESTROYER...

J.M.THORNTON

ROYAL YACHTS AS NAVAL AUXILIARIES

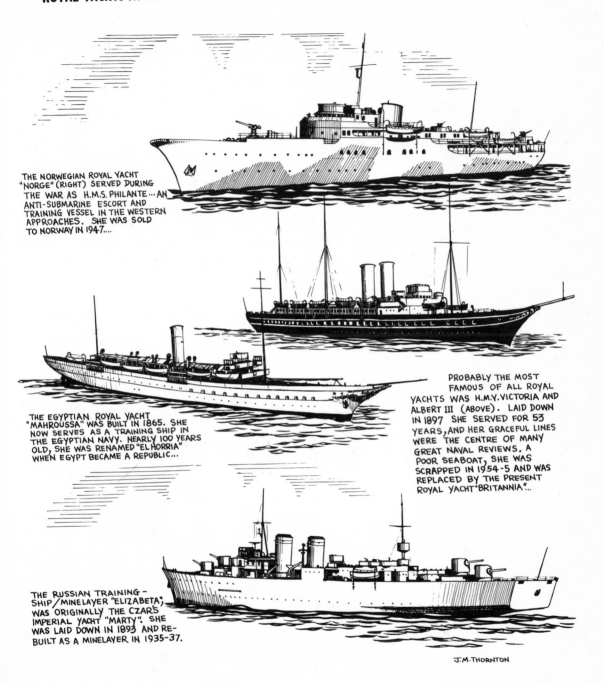

THE NORWEGIAN ROYAL YACHT "NORGE" (RIGHT) SERVED DURING THE WAR AS H.M.S. PHILANTE... AN ANTI-SUBMARINE ESCORT AND TRAINING VESSEL IN THE WESTERN APPROACHES. SHE WAS SOLD TO NORWAY IN 1947....

THE EGYPTIAN ROYAL YACHT "MAHROUSSA" WAS BUILT IN 1865. SHE NOW SERVES AS A TRAINING SHIP IN THE EGYPTIAN NAVY. NEARLY 100 YEARS OLD, SHE WAS RENAMED "EL HORRIA" WHEN EGYPT BECAME A REPUBLIC...

PROBABLY THE MOST FAMOUS OF ALL ROYAL YACHTS WAS H.M.Y. VICTORIA AND ALBERT III (ABOVE). LAID DOWN IN 1897 SHE SERVED FOR 53 YEARS, AND HER GRACEFUL LINES WERE THE CENTRE OF MANY GREAT NAVAL REVIEWS. A POOR SEABOAT, SHE WAS SCRAPPED IN 1954-5 AND WAS REPLACED BY THE PRESENT ROYAL YACHT "BRITANNIA"...

THE RUSSIAN TRAINING-SHIP/MINELAYER "ELIZABETA", WAS ORIGINALLY THE CZAR'S IMPERIAL YACHT "MARTY". SHE WAS LAID DOWN IN 1893 AND RE-BUILT AS A MINELAYER IN 1935-37.

J.M. THORNTON

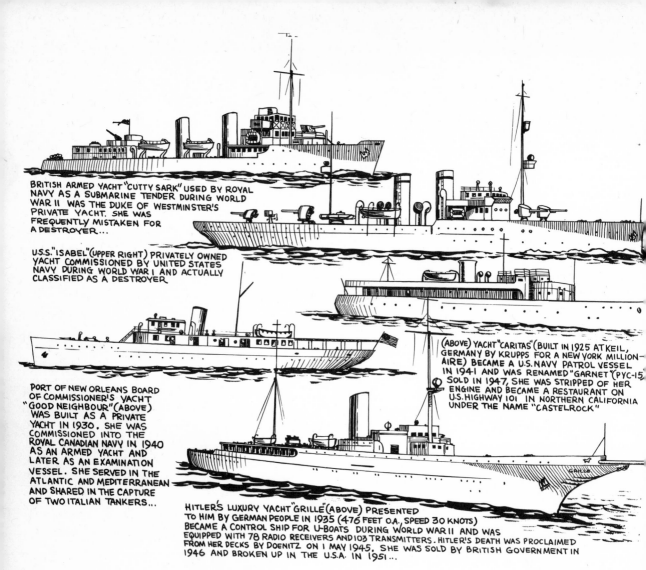

BRITISH ARMED YACHT "CUTTY SARK" USED BY ROYAL NAVY AS A SUBMARINE TENDER DURING WORLD WAR II WAS THE DUKE OF WESTMINSTER'S PRIVATE YACHT. SHE WAS FREQUENTLY MISTAKEN FOR A DESTROYER...

U.S.S. "ISABEL" (UPPER RIGHT) PRIVATELY OWNED YACHT COMMISSIONED BY UNITED STATES NAVY DURING WORLD WAR I AND ACTUALLY CLASSIFIED AS A DESTROYER

(ABOVE) YACHT "CARITAS" (BUILT IN 1925 AT KEIL, GERMANY BY KRUPPS FOR A NEW YORK MILLIONAIRE) BECAME A U.S. NAVY PATROL VESSEL IN 1941 AND WAS RENAMED "GARNET" (PYC-15) SOLD IN 1947, SHE WAS STRIPPED OF HER ENGINE AND BECAME A RESTAURANT ON U.S. HIGHWAY 101 IN NORTHERN CALIFORNIA UNDER THE NAME "CASTELROCK"

PORT OF NEW ORLEANS BOARD OF COMMISSIONER'S YACHT "GOOD NEIGHBOUR" (ABOVE) WAS BUILT AS A PRIVATE YACHT IN 1930. SHE WAS COMMISSIONED INTO THE ROYAL CANADIAN NAVY IN 1940 AS AN ARMED YACHT AND LATER AS AN EXAMINATION VESSEL. SHE SERVED IN THE ATLANTIC AND MEDITERRANEAN AND SHARED IN THE CAPTURE OF TWO ITALIAN TANKERS...

HITLER'S LUXURY YACHT "GRILLE" (ABOVE) PRESENTED TO HIM BY GERMAN PEOPLE IN 1935 (476 FEET O.A., SPEED 30 KNOTS) BECAME A CONTROL SHIP FOR U-BOATS DURING WORLD WAR II AND WAS EQUIPPED WITH 78 RADIO RECEIVERS AND 103 TRANSMITTERS. HITLER'S DEATH WAS PROCLAIMED FROM HER DECKS BY DOENITZ ON 1 MAY 1945. SHE WAS SOLD BY BRITISH GOVERNMENT IN 1946 AND BROKEN UP IN THE U.S.A. IN 1951...

J.M. THORNTON